THE FOLLOWING DISCLAIMERS APPLY TO ALL CONTENT WITHIN THIS BOOK. THE SAME DISCLAIMERS APPLY, WHETHER MATERIAL IS QUOTED, DUPLICATED AND CREDITED TO THE BOOK OR NOT.

The opinions voiced in this book are for general information only and are not intended to provide specific advice or recommendations for any individual.

Investing involves risk including loss of principal.

There is no guarantee that a diversified portfolio will enhance overall returns or outperform a non-diversified portfolio. Diversification does not protect against market risk.

All performance referenced is historical and is no guarantee of future results.

All indices are unmanaged and may not be invested into directly. No strategy assures success or protects against loss.

Prior to investing in a 529 Plan investors should consider whether the investor's or designated beneficiary's home state offers any state tax or other state benefits such as financial aid, scholarship funds, and protection from creditors that are only available for investments in such state's qualified tuition program. Withdrawals used for qualified expenses are federally tax free. Tax treatment at the state level may vary. Please consult with your tax advisor before investing.

Examples are hypothetical and not representative of any specific situation. Your results will vary. The hypothetical rates of return used do not reflect the deduction of fees and charges inherent to investing.

This information is not intended to be a substitute for specific individualized tax advice. We suggest that you discuss your specific tax issues with a qualified tax advisor.

The Dow Jones Industrial Average is comprised of 30 stocks that are major factors in their industries and widely held by individuals and institutional investors.

Peter Mullin is a financial consultant, currently registered through LPL Financial.

This book, or any owner as assign, and LPL Financial are separate entities.

Securities and Advisory services offered through LPL Financial, a Registered Investment Advisor. Member FINRA/SIPC.

FALSE
Financial Finish Lines

●●●

Pursue a Comfortable Life Now and Through Retirement

PETER MULLIN

Financial Author

Copyright © 2018.

False Financial Finish Lines.
Pursue a Comfortable Life Now and Through Retirement.
Copyright © 2018 by Peter Mullin. ALL RIGHTS RESERVED. No part of this book may be used or reproduced in any manner whatsoever without written permission except in the case of brief quotations. For information, address Peter Mullin.

ISBN-13: 978-1727243826
ISBN-10: 172724382X

False Financial Finish Lines

CONTENTS

Introduction: Your Wealth Journey • 3

1: Pursue a Self-Controlled Retirement • 9
2: Retirement is a Noun • 15
3: The Road to Retirement:
   While You Were Busy Living • 24
4: How Do You Measure Up? • 30
5: Family • 40
6: Education:
   Helping Your Ducklings Cross the Road • 46
7: Careers • 50
8: Your Home • 53
9: Entrepreneurs: The Independent Path • 61
10: The Physician's Journey • 69
11: Measure Twice, Retire Once • 79
12: Living in Retirement: Don't Burst The Balloon • 87
13: Aging Gracefully • 93

Appendix • 99
References

False Financial Finish Lines

Introduction — Your Wealth Journey

What if you filled a ship plump full with gold coins, then sunk that ship in the sea, and never told anyone? Would those gold coins have any worth?

A goldsmith can shape gold into fantastic things. But all that glitters is not gold.

Gold means nothing to a baby. Let a one-year-old hold a bag filled with gold coins, and that child will still look at you with pure love. Give that same bag of gold to an adult, and they may imagine all sorts of things they may do and buy with it

What's wealth to you?

When will you have enough?

Money is a bold topic. Some cringe when the subject comes up. For others, it's a favorite past-time.

What's your relationship with money?

This is what I've come to learn: Wealth is relative. Retirement is a noun. You fill in the blanks.

Wealth is not all about money. Nor is retirement a life of golf courses and long breakfasts. Sure these activities can be a part of yours. Wealth accumulates in both rich experiences and hopefully assets.

False Financial Finish Lines

Wealth is the result of hard work and persistence. You forge wealth with healthy habits and unique life experiences. Just as soon as you think you achieved some imagined milestone, you realize there is more to pursue in front of you.

Your wealth is often guided by your gut more than your mind — more than you may like to admit.

Sports psychologists say that to become an expert at a sport you need to practice it very often.

So that's what I do; I practice my craft daily. I have listened to stories about individuals that may be a little like you. I read — a lot. I observe.

I share ideas that can have a positive impact on you and many others.

I draw on Nobel Prize-winning ideas. Concepts like diversification, and how you can make sound choices more easily. If you're curious about what I read, then look up Nobel Laureates like Harry Maslow, Richard Thaler, and Robert Shiller.

I hear, see, and read the same marketing material that you do. In fact, I would wager that I see far more of it than you do. Or at least I pay attention to it. I have an eye and ear for it.

Take for example a college student. They quit doing something they enjoyed because it cost them money. The stress of expenses from textbooks and tuition caused them to stop doing what brought them joy. Even if that bit of pleasure came from a rare mocha treat.

Perhaps you are retired and are still concerned about running low on money — even though your professionals have told you, they think you're okay.

False Financial Finish Lines

I know how many parts of the personal financial wealth story work together. Parts of your prosperity puzzle get left out. And if you miss one piece? Well, the puzzle doesn't look complete. The missing or neglected pieces can cause problems. At 35, a couple would rather pay off a 6% student loan than invest in their 401(k). But at 60, that same couple would rather have more saved for retirement.

Paying off debt instead of funding retirement can be seen as a financial contradiction. Or is it?

I've heard so many stories about folks who are trying to get their money to behave for them. I've seen plenty take what I felt was thoughtful pro bono advice ... and do the opposite.

Transitions and changes cause us to panic or stress.

We use the fight or flight response. It could benefit many of us to become aware of this. We don't like uncertain times and changes in life. We resist or avoid decisions that could help us in the long run. It's easier to do nothing. This is complacency. The gym membership you do not use, and subscription services rely on us not taking action. We are lazy.

We become preoccupied with protecting our money and feeling comfortable. We ignore sound advice because specific life events and choices paralyze us.

Your life story can shape your wealth. Many things can cause the Scale of Wealth to shift for you. Change knocks with job transitions, new business ventures, moving, and family. Change can be scary. Life can get busy.

A job change, in particular, can be the scariest of transitions. Especially that final job change before retirement. We do tend to define ourselves by what we do. And our paychecks support our life. So when our careers shift it can become a crisis that hijacks choices we make.

Money changes hands. Time can heal. But abrupt changes in life are abrupt because they often aren't announced.

I divided this book into three parts.

Part One consists of chapters one through four. These chapters begin to describe several ways to think about retirement. Again, a helpful way to think of retirement is as a life event – not some finish line. No. It's a transition. Moreover, once you retire, you know that life continues to transition as you age.

Part Two consists of chapters five through thirteen. These chapters discuss life and the false finish lines that exist in our lives. As you get older, you find that life isn't as easy as when you were young. You achieve one milestone, and you look up and — if you're lucky — you still see a long road in front of you.

The day you were born, the world was already checking your achievements off. You roll over your first time. Your first word. You learn to ride a bike. Then you're graduating one grade at a time.

You grow up with questions like, "What do you want to be when you grow up?" And our young selves learn in this way that it's healthy to have an answer.

My first significant moments of independence arrived after college. After college, I learned that you continue to navigate a world full of finish lines in your career. This chapter talks about these life events. They happen as you progress toward retirement, of course.

I included chapters about physicians and entrepreneurs. I am familiar with these life journeys. I also happen to think that there are many habits that we can borrow from some of the hardest working folks around. To learn about delayed gratification, ask your doctor about her educational journey. If you want to gain real work ethic, then ask a farmer if you can help him for one week.

Life is busy. And on your best days, it seems like life goes by so fast. Cherish those good days.

Part Three is the *Appendix*. The *Appendix* shares the same name as a part of our bowels that we don't need to survive. Yet it can cause a great deal of trouble if it flares up. So that's what these topics are. They are topics – important ones – that arise in conversation. And if you don't pay close attention, it may cause a good deal of financial pain later.

This Appendix is like a potluck dinner for financial goals and FAQs. If you've been to a potluck, you know that dinner is always a surprise. You bring enough food for you and your family. And you share amongst friends and family.

So, what should you bring to this part of the book? Curiosity and a mind full of questions. Are there questions you want to examine for the benefit of your family?

I've left this chapter for last because it's one you could page through when you want to go into more detail. As a professional, I hear a lot of questions about the latest news headlines. *How will this affect your portfolio?* Debt management is another popular topic. Finally, there are those who want to learn more about spending from a portfolio. How do you create retirement income from your portfolio?

So welcome and congratulations. A book about finance is a bold undertaking for me. It seems to become a preferred topic when things flare up in our life. By reading on, I hope you'll feel inclined to redefine your vision of wealth and retirement.

And I think that would be a good goal.

This book is about building momentum.

It's about building confidence in your life and wealth. It's about what's next. It's about revisiting what's essential in both the near-term and the long-term for you.

Our families and lives all have the potential to be beautiful. They are no longer things to check off a list. When you get your finances in alignment, there's more room to sit back and enjoy.

So, welcome, friend. May you enjoy a prosperous life.

Pursue a Self-Controlled Retirement

In 1960, a child was sat down in a chair. Her mom and the man with glasses smiled at her.

The man in glasses set a marshmallow in front of her. He told her, "If you don't eat this before we return, then we'll be sure to get you another marshmallow. Just ring this bell if you need us, and we'll be right here."

The door closed and the child crossed her arms on the table in front of her. The stare down began. It continued as they watched the child from another room.

The man in glasses ran this experiment over and over again with different children. The children had mixed results. Some ate the one marshmallow straight away. Others did not. They waited for the return of the man with glasses and their mom. The kids who didn't eat the marshmallow got an extra marshmallow, as promised.

And so this is how the destiny of children came to be. Through a test of grit with marshmallows. Marshmallows were like a fortuneteller. The sugary treat foretold children's potential prosperity.

Now how does a marshmallow foretell destiny? Okay. This interpretation is dramatic. But the preschoolers experienced a test of willpower. And willpower, you will find, can be the difference between maxing out a 401(k) this year or not. It can be the difference between saying no to an expensive car loan. And these little financial tests of willpower can build up over time.

Professor Walter Mischel's experiment is often referred to as, "The Marshmallow Test." He shared his results in 1972. Mischel wanted to use a simple study to measure something much more meaningful.

Mischel and others studied the results of his Marshmallow Test. They contacted some of the children who participated in the experiment later in their young adulthood. Those who had the willpower to stare down one sugary treat, were likely to experience success in life. These kids obtained high college entry scores, performed better in college, and earned higher incomes.

The children who went ahead and ate the marshmallow generally did not do as well in college and life.

This is an experiment that gets told time and time again. It is a classic example of how living one way today can help you achieve something tomorrow. It's a story of consequences and how simple things shape our lives for later.

It's the story of how a child may prove early on whether he or she understands the advantages of waiting.

So?

What's a marshmallow have to do with your retirement?

Actually, an immense amount.

Unfortunately, retirement in the United States is still very much self-controlled. The good news is that you chose to read this book. Other anecdotes that reference the Marshmallow Test aren't for preschoolers. It's for you to pay attention to and develop from.

Retirement for you is self-controlled. That means it's your responsibility.

Most of us like to feel that we are in control. But it turns out that a self-controlled retirement may not be a good thing. We fool ourselves into thinking we make good choices. Some Nobel Prize-winning ideas and more tell us otherwise.

What about social security and pensions? Sure they exist. Old-fashioned pensions can help support your lifestyle in retirement. But remember, they are programs that you pay toward. Money is withheld from your paycheck. You will find that there is more than one resource to help fund your lifestyle in retirement.

What's your lifestyle like today? Are you comfortable? It may be one of great privilege. Or do you wonder how your friends manage to do so well when you feel like your family is trying to keep up?

What do balanced lifestyles, comfort, and sound financial sense all have in common? They take perspective and good habits. It takes a willingness to learn and develop. It takes discipline.

I've learned that there are three types of aspiring retirees. There are those who have true disadvantages that may be perpetuated by low income and poor education. There is the average, disciplined human. Finally, there are outliers. Those who make a ton of dough but spend too much and can't keep track of where it all goes. There is another subset of outliers. Those who seem to accumulate wealth with outward ease – kind of like average, disciplined humans. These accumulators possess a backstory of grit, passion, and discipline.

False Financial Finish Lines

When you approach the retirement finish line, what habits will you have developed along the way? How can you use your education and habits to contribute to a comfortable retirement?

Your lifestyle is unique. The Marshmallow Test may tell us that we all get a fair shot at building a firm financial foundation.

You can stare down the marshmallow.

Some things seem to put the odds against us. Yes, the one who has a higher income has more money to invest and save. However, the person with limited or average financial resources often has the edge when it comes to saving for retirement. These families tend to develop a conservative money mindset and good financial habits.

It's an idea of biblical proportions: "Whoever can be trusted with very little can also be trusted with much." (Luke 16:10)

It's always easier to improve your lifestyle than to consume less. If you're used to macaroni and cheese, then you might enjoy linguine. But if you grew up with linguine, then mac and cheese may not be your favorite.

Your lifestyle and retirement are unique. Many messages may suggest otherwise. What age should you claim social security? When will you have enough saved? It's like there's a magic portfolio value where we all the sudden have the means.

Take your time. Get to know your retirement numbers. Take the time to appreciate your circumstances. You'll recognize when you are ready.

False Financial Finish Lines

Your journey will be different from your friends. It's like two friends going to the lake to swim. Some jump off the dock straight into the deep end. You may prefer to wade in and get your feet wet, first.

Where does this difference in means and lifestyle begin?

It's like those preschoolers who took part in a study of willpower and marshmallows.

Understand what you can control to improve your lifestyle. You can make small decisions today to try and enhance your retirement.

If you begin with small goals, your reward can sustain you.

What if you saved $90,000 when you were 30? If that money got an annual return of 7%, it could be worth about $1,190,000 by the time you turned 67.

Also, did you know that the future value of $1,000,000 could erode to about 1/3 of that much due to inflation? The cost of buying stuff goes up after 37 years.

Did you also know that personal finance books written in the 1970's used a cool million dollars as a grand goal? A million dollars sounds cool. But it's a number.

Your retirement is so very personal compared to your friends and those around you. If you are healthy, employed, and educated, then you are well equipped to control your future.

It's your life. It's your money.

This book is about expectations. It's about addressing the false financial goals that exist. Think. Then act. Think about your money. Think about what retirement is. Think about your transition into retirement. Think about your life. Think about life when you're no longer with your family.

Then act to shape your life. You can do a lot in a lifetime.

Bill Gates helps put time into perspective. He says, "Most people overestimate what they can do in one year and underestimate what they can do in ten years."

When you finish reading this book, are you going to walk away and eat the marshmallow? Or will you reframe financial finish lines for yourself?

Start thinking about what you can do in five and ten years. What can you do in 20 years?

Harness a different mindset. There is much that will distract you. There is always something distracting you from your end goals. Maxing out a 401(k) does not sound like fun. Driving a new car sure does. The sugar in marshmallows is addictive. The brain loves sugar. But the brain needs other nutrients to sustain itself.

And sure life is short and you ought to enjoy it. But how will you fuel your retirement? How will you fuel the next change in your life?

So?

Are you ready to stare down the retirement marshmallow with me?

Retirement Is a Noun

Retirement: a. an act of *retiring*:
the state of being *retired*.

Crossing the retirement finish line can be anti-climatic. It is like an Olympic athlete arriving home to their apartment after taking home gold. They've trained their entire life to live that moment on the pedestal. Their anthem plays while their flag flies above the other nation's. This moment is theirs. The fanfare may continue with TV shows and interviews.

But then the noise turns down, and folks move on to other things. I imagine this like a sugar rush. The hype and energy are there. Then it's not. Information and trending news moves as fast as our thumbs and fingers can tap on our devices.

How did the Beatles get so big? They had no internet. They flew on slow planes.

Imagine Abraham Lincoln getting his message out through the telegraph and train. What if he had social media? Word moves fast today. A response to an opponent back then must have taken 3-7 days!

People have moved on by then.

I remember moving on from high school and college. These were significant events in my mind. Then life moved on.

False Financial Finish Lines

My high school and college were on the same beautiful campus. High school was right up the hill from the college campus. From the interstate, you can see the lofty concrete bell-banner tower. You used to take the old entry to Saint John's University through the pine trees. You might have had about a one-mile stretch of bumpy road in front of you.

Today you enter the 2,000-acre campus on a beautiful road. You see a prairie preserve to one side and an old farmstead on the other. I graduated and exited this campus and immersive environment twice. Both times my windows were down. The prairie and pine-infused wind rushed in around me, and champion music played. I had a world of opportunity ahead.

Life changes can be thrilling.

A friend gave me a card at my Confirmation. He selected a card and quote from Robert Frost. Frost tells us, "I can sum up everything I've learned about life in three words: It moves on." At the time I didn't appreciate it. How could I? I was young! I hadn't experienced the ups and downs of life. I had no idea of financial responsibility. I didn't appreciate what it felt like to move on.

I don't know about you, but every graduation season since, I look up famous graduation speeches. Look up great speeches yourself. It reinvigorates you and can be nostalgic. The speakers highlight life values, dreams, and ambition. They all have the typical outlines like this:

Congratulations! It took a lot to get here.

Be mindful of your internal compass as you move forward.

Keep your dreams close.

False Financial Finish Lines

You will have challenges.
Here is a personal story about that.
Go forth and pursue your dreams!

There is no pomp and circumstance for your retirement. Sure there are corporate parties; you can throw a party yourself. But soon the music of your career will dial down.

And who will you be the next morning? What will your story be moving forward?

Life moves on. And fast.

If your only goal is retirement for retirement's sake, then pay attention. If you have goals like crocheting or fishing, then pay attention.

Here's a brief English lesson for us: "Retirement," is a noun. It is a word that describes something or someone.

I am a dad. "Dad," is a noun. But it doesn't describe something. It conjures up all sorts of ideas. Usually, these are ideas based on your exposure to dads in your life. It's the same for retirement. What kind of plans does retirement conjure up for you?

Retirement is not an active word. It's a blank slate. It can be thrilling. Have you ever painted from a blank slate or created something from scratch? Have you ever cooked something without a recipe?

A blank slate can be intimidating. But for many that blank canvas fills in quick with hobbies and friends. Retired folks explain that they are, "Busier than ever." That's great! Enjoy your good years.

Retirement is a transition. Once you are there, it continues to transform. New Zealand funded a study via the Commission for Financial Capability. It helps define aging and living in retirement in three stages.

The first part of retirement is what's thought of as your Active Years or Discovery. Discovery is a time retirees often describe as busy.

Discovery is a stage in financial planning, too. It's the part where we learn all about you. You share what's most important to you and what you want to develop in your financial life. It's about your goals and the time horizon you have for trying to reach your goals.

So you could discover your retirement story in the same way. It's like the Olympic athlete returning home. They trained their entire life. They won. Now, what's next?

If you've raised a family, then this part of life could be about exploring passions that you have put to the side. You can hear yourself think. That's new, too! Is it about doing more of what you love with your free time? What passions do you have? The blank slate fills in quick.

Hobbies and activities cost money. Spending money on enriching leisure during your young retirement years is normal. Yet spending money may be intimidating. For spending can cause some discomfort.

Your financial goals before retirement were about growing money. And paying debts.

What happens when your paychecks stop? Now you have a dependency on the money you've stored away for later.

Now you are spending money that you have saved. It's a 180-degree change. It can be jarring. You're now spending cash and investments without restocking the money you spend.

False Financial Finish Lines

Remember, the third part of this book will zoom in on areas like spending your money. For now, realize that this is familiar territory for retirement studies and scholars. We assume you want to spend your retirement money and you want it to sustain you for your lifetime.

But it is common to fear running out of money. This fear can start to settle in at least a decade before you retire. Do you have enough saved? How are you doing? This fear plays softly in the background for some. It is loud and at the forefront of others. It can cause you to do bizarre things with your money. It can cause you to mess up a sound strategy.

A natural fear is that you will spend too much early on. It reminds me of the cavemen who went through quite a lot to hunt and bring food home.

When you are getting low on something, you tend to eat less of it. Preservation is in our DNA.

This past summer we went on a camping trip in Voyageurs National Park. It was only a two-night trip. We had several means of cleaning lake water, so it was safe to drink. But we brought a large bladder of water and 5-gallons of tap water from home. After two days of paddling in rough waters, we still had about half of the 5-gallons of water left. The final morning was calm. Before we packed out, we were generous with our water portions and cleaning methods. The end of our trip was near, and we'd soon be around tap water, again.

So we did not run out of tap water on our brief canoe trip. We had brought more than enough with us.

Retirement planning strives to create a blueprint for your money. What money will you spend first? How much of your money should you withdraw? How dependent will you be on your investments? Planning can help limit the fear of "eating or drinking too much" of your wealth. Of course, you have unknowns.

Since 2008, I have seen a rush of marketing that attempts to interpret and provide solutions to this fear.

Running out of money is a rational concern. It should be even more concerning if you do not have great habits. Investors take actions that 'screw up' portfolios. They panic. Instead of following a charted course they try and take shortcuts and run aground.

Then you may have healthy habits. Your habits may translate to spending too little.

The preservation mentality works for most of us. It seems natural to take evasive action to preserve what you have. I've read about places that are living in a real drought. They need to limit their water use in places like Cape Town, South Africa. It's scary. And yet, folks are continuing to use too much water.

And let me clarify that I don't think money is a life and death matter. But that is my point. Water is something you need to survive. So in the face of drought, our behaviors should change.

Water is such a profound resource. And people are still neglecting the warnings.

This same behavior shows up when retirees spend too much and are at risk of running out. It happens with inheritances more often than you may think, also. It occurs when an employee cashes out a "small" retirement account when they leave a business. It happens when people cash out retirement accounts to buy things they want today. It occurs when an inheritance disappears in a couple of years or less.

So keep reminding your family and neighbors to not to eat the marshmallow. Delay some comfort today. Exchange it for some comfort tomorrow.

The current retired generation tends to have the "Camping with Tap Water," mentality.

This fear of running out can lead to spending too little on yourself. How is that possible? I've heard many reasons why. Usually, it is due to healthcare costs or a strong desire to leave a legacy with the next generations.

Do you have senior parents who have amassed wealth? You can't coach them to spend much on themselves. Right?

The habits that help you develop wealth will likely follow you into retirement. That is a good thing.

I guess I'd rather be conservative in my spending than frivolous. Clients don't tell me, "I wish we saved less for retirement."

The story of our camping trip to Voyageurs National Park is likely foreshadowing for me. It helps me realize some traits about myself.

I've used another image that involves water with clients. It's the idea of filling a giant water balloon up with water – saving for retirement. Then in retirement, the game changes. Then we're left to determine where to place a pinprick in that balloon so that water flows and can try and sustain you.

It's an intimidating concept. Have you ever poked a full balloon? It pops! In the case of a water balloon, water bursts out. All you have are the remnants of the balloon.

Most retirees like to preserve their water.

Retirement companies have caught on. Have you noticed your employer's 401(k) statement show you how much income you might expect when you retire? There's a reason for this. Observe the disclaimers. But this is in part because a lump sum of money is a number. There's value in imagining how your portfolio will generate income for you in retirement.

So what if you have $250,000 …. $500,000 … $2-million saved for retirement? These are false finish lines. They are round numbers. How much will you spend from year to year? That's of far greater importance. And consequence. If you spend $5,000 a month will you have enough to get you to the end of life?

It's a proper perspective. Your retirement portfolio is a resource for lifelong income. When do you plan to run out?

Bring this thought into social security claims. When should you claim social security?

You don't need to reinvent the wheel. We need to acknowledge potential challenges and select reasonably reliable strategies.

You may have benefited from decades of investing a portion of your paycheck. Now it'd be nice to automatically take money out to live off of for the rest of your life. Retirement income automation is not here – yet. At least it's not universal. But it's close.

Living in retirement brings many changes. It's natural to wonder what it will be like. After a long road up to retirement, I wish for you to feel well informed and financially prepared.

False Financial Finish Lines

Camping and water analogies aside, retirement is a life to look forward to. Don't strive to reinvent the wheel. Strive for a comfortable retirement by becoming an informed investor. Discuss all your options with your professionals. Then enjoy.

The Road to Retirement:
While You Were Busy Living

"Life is what happens to you while you are busy making other plans."
-Allen Saunders, Readers Digest

Focus now on the events, distractions, and good habits that accumulate before your version of retirement.

Retirement is a self-controlled lifestyle for many of us in the United States. This is because we don't have much in the way of financial support to sustain us through retirement. Pensions are for the minority of workers – especially in the 21st century. Social security benefits are limited to a portion of what you earned during your average years.

Not to mention that between your graduation from high school and your imagined retirement age, there is a very, very wide divide.

This time can work for you if you study the history of investing in stocks and what compounding interest can do for you. But it also introduces this thing called life. You have marriage, businesses, careers homes, children, college, job changes, new roofs, moves, hospital bills, vacations, cars, and all sorts of priorities between here and retirement.

False Financial Finish Lines

These are life events. Many of these events help us interact and love those around us more. They help add meaning to life. It's the here and now. Other events cause real pain and can draw us inward.

There are countless things that we can buy today that make us feel good. I can buy the latest greatest tech gadget. I can hold a gadget. I can surf the web. The information and things we desire can be ours in nearly an instant.

Progress toward financial goals can feel like a glacier slowly sliding down a mountain. You may not realize your goals in years or even decades. Your money goals surely will not be accomplished overnight. Longterm financial results are undervalued. The instant gratification is not there. Compounding interest can work wonders over decades. If you watch your money day-to-day, it will be assuredly dull. A news headline or famous personality can cause us to question what we're doing.

You may become passionate about a short-term financial goal. You may have a wedding to pay for and a checklist of 101 things to do before the wedding. Once a date is marked on the calendar, then the Save the Date cards must go in the mail. The list is long and can be daunting. But you check the items of the list with enthusiasm. The clock is ticking. And soon the great day will arrive.

Hey, the clock is ticking for your children. How will you purchase a quality education for them? Retirement is a few decades or at least years away. Life experiences can fuel your mindful saving. But when was the last time you got super excited about your financial plan?

It's no wonder living in retirement is a goal that we tend to neglect. After all, retirement is kind of ambiguous, right?

Pain and joy are real feelings. We experience them while we're busy living.

But retirement is a noun. Retirement is relative.

It's not active. It's ambiguous.

You need to have some imagination or a great role model to inspire you to care for your financial future. Good financial habits can reap great reward when discovered early in life.

Use Your Imagination

You'll need imagination because you won't believe you're going to be 80 some day.

You ought to look at your parents and ask them if they ever thought they would have children and be where they are today. Then, if you're lucky enough to have grandparents, go ahead and ask them the same. Did they ever imagine they would age? What do they know about aging gracefully?

Life goes by fast. It couldn't hurt to ask someone who is 20, 30, or 50 years your senior about their experience.

There's a lot of value that our seniors add to society. Spending time with grandparents and seniors may cause you to see aging differently. Try it. You may just lift the spirits of someone who really values your company. And you may benefit from their wisdom.

What I learned about wealth came mostly from books. I also had unrecognized role-models in my childhood: my parents.

False Financial Finish Lines

My wife can thank my mom for my habit of keeping clothes a decade too long. I enjoy a new suit every few years. But my mom was always stretching one dollar into ten for our family of 13. Incredible.

The rest of my childhood personal finance education came from tidbits of advice from my dad. He sat down with me once or twice with spreadsheets. Many other times he stressed that I should split the money I made from a paper route 50/50. I should save half of my paycheck and then I could spend the other half.

Silly me. I actually listened! At times I saved more than half.

So I continued to do this with my high school jobs. Then I proceeded to save through college, and the habit has carried on.

I think it would be impressive to live on half your earned wage. But life happens.

I think kids are genuinely open to financial tips — more than parents and grandparents realize. Kids may not sit down and read an entire book. But they are paying attention. I think if children hear about good money habits early, they're more inclined to test those habits out. Then maybe, just maybe, the good habits will actually stick!

My good habit to save sometimes got noticed by friends. I once "lent" money to someone. They paid me back with old things they no longer wanted or new stuff I didn't need. I learned not to give my money away so freely.

My habit of saving matured into investing. My dad, again, showed me with three columns on a very simple spreadsheet. This was the power of compounding interest. He taught me that this is how much I could make in savings. This is what I could make in a CD. This is what I could make investing. That was how I learned about compounding interest. It looked like a snowball rolling downhill. It just accumulated. Each column had different measures of risk attached.

> *"Compound interest is the eighth wonder of the world. He who understands it, earns it ... he who doesn't ... pays it." -*
> *Albert Einstein*

My dad taught me about investing and basic budgeting and saving with brief anecdotes. My mom showed us how to budget and stretch a dollar. I think that's called "thrifty" – a part of the Scout Law.

The idea of saving has stuck. It has matured into investing and caring for my own family.

Sure we all would love to be millionaires or feel comfortable in retirement. But life and wealth are relative. The good news is that some financial choices are self-controlled and in your hands. We all would love to be the recipient of a 30 or 50-year investment. The good news? You likely can be. You have to start on day #1 and live out good habits.

You can experience beautiful events on the road to retirement.

Life and retirement can be in harmony. You just need to mind your resources along the way.

So look for inspiration. Look for motivation within silly ads on TV or a lunch presentation at work. Find motivation online and in books. Retirement is a self-controlled goal for many of us.

False Financial Finish Lines

Life will happen. Something will always be vying for your attention and your money. Take the time now to prepare for the known events that can come up.

Things like houses, cars, education bills all pull on your emergency reserves. It often happens when you just thought you were ahead. Remember: It's always something.

If one life event sets you back, then go back to your good financial habits. Rebuild your emergency cash reserves and carry on.

How Do You Measure Up?

Congratulations!

Your numbers say you can retire. That's good news!

You've spent the past 15-years observing your financial statements. You know different modes of income like social security will take the place of your paycheck. You are aware of how you may try to maximize your various ways of obtaining money to live off.

If the numbers say so, then you may as well go straight for the retirement finish line, right?

Not so fast.

What is retirement for you? Many are quick to explain, "I've never been busier [than in retirement]!" But what will define your retirement? What will drive you?

There is a measurable amount of the population that would be wise to pay attention to themselves. Titles and responsibilities seem to accumulate with age. It can be easy to lose sight of yourself with children, work, and business. You know the feeling?

The goal of this chapter is to help you realize how you imagine retirement today. And then you can start to shape it for tomorrow. Begin to define retirement with intent. Perhaps you'll find inspiration in personalizing the word for you and your family.

When will you retire? What will you do when you do retire? What will you do if you make it to 90? What would you want to be said at your eulogy?

Retirement for many translates to no work life. You can wake up without an alarm clock. You can spend more time with friends and family. You spent a lifetime to get a to a point where you could cross that finish line called "retirement." What will the first weeks look like? What will the first three years look like? What will retirement later look like after 15 years?

The first job that offered you a retirement plan introduced you to save for retirement. Living in retirement is a primary, long-term financial goal for many investors. You placed money in your company retirement plan. If you have had the fortune of doing this long enough, you hopefully started to amass an amount of money.

You may have watched your first $1,000 accumulate. Then you went for $25,000...$50,000, $100,000, $250,000...

Now what? You're retiring, and it's time to think different. It's typical for retirees to begin to think about portfolio preservation. This is especially true if you have a high dependency on the money.

Let's take inventory of your retirement livelihood.

There are various ways to measure your retirement goal. You could determine when you are all set for your retirement in three ways or a combination of these three ways:

1. Retirement by Numbers: You can review your numbers with (often free) retirement calculators. You could get more specific with a financial and/or tax professional – I think you should.

2. Retirement by Benefit: You could retire when you reach your full retirement age, according to social security benefits. You might do the same when you are eligible for a traditional pension benefit.

3. Retirement as a Transition: You view retirement as a transition. It's a season to live out life goals and passions. This is my current retirement philosophy. Does this mean an encore career? Would this involve providing childcare for your grandchildren? Could this mean assisting with non-profit organizations you've become familiar with?

Retirement by Numbers

Retirement by Numbers is measuring all your money and assets and modes of retirement income. In your working years, this money is a long stick with a carrot attached to it.

Are you saying (or have you said) *no* to enough of your money today to receive benefits from it years from now?

Retirement calculators come down to numbers.

It's a simple idea of money in and money out. How much money will you be able to live comfortably from? How much will you accumulate to live life with confidence?

What are you planning to spend in a month of retirement? $3000? $5000? $20,000?

There are plenty of details that you should be aware of. You can review retirement calculators – often free ones – and get different results. Remember, a calculator takes the information you give it, and provides the arithmetical answer. Understand what you are saying to the calculator. Know what the calculator is trying to tell you. Observe the disclaimers. Does that make sense?

There are plenty of rules of thumb to guide you.

But is a rule of thumb the prudent way to guide your retirement? Rules of thumb educate and guide the public. Rules of thumb make an effort to simplify things.

Be smart. Realize a rule of thumb is like a billboard or newspaper advertisement. There's usually more to the story.

Can a rule of thumb apply to you? Yes. Before going further, please consider the following:

Here's the definition from Merriam-Webster (merriam-webster.com) :

Rule of Thumb: 1. a method of procedure based on experience and common sense; 2. a general principle regarded as roughly correct but not intended to be scientifically accurate.

It's that part about, "not intended to be scientifically accurate," that causes me to pause.

Rules of Thumb in personal finance have been born out of a desire to motivate and educate.

When we have a sick child, we can refer to the web for general information as a guide. Nurse lines exist today for the same reason. Yet, when our child is sick, and we need trusted help, we're advised to go to the doctor, and the ER if it's an emergency.

The trouble with a rule of thumb is the many important disclaimers. The disclaimers try to describe consequences.

Unfortunately, disclaimers are easy to overlook ... or ignore.

The financial answer you're looking for often depends on your situation. So you best call upon a professional to provide customized guidance. Indeed, a rule of thumb or generic calculator may motivate you to begin to save more for retirement.

Retirement by Benefit

You know you're a senior when you can get your senior coffee pricing and other discounts. You know you're a senior when AARP knows your name and where you live. You know you've made it as a senior when information about Medicare starts to arrive in your mailbox.

Society provides many reminders of retirement finish lines. Some examples are pensions and social security benefits.

What supports a retirement lifestyle?

To make a tricycle go, you need three wheels. Right?

Two financial wheels for retirees are pensions and your investments. The third supplemental wheel is your social security benefit.

The great thing about Social Security is it has done a part of the retirement savings job for you. You don't need to review your investment menu through work. You don't need to listen to a financial professional give lengthy explanations.

But it provides a false finish line. It says you can be ready to claim as early as 62 or 63. You can eat the marshmallow. Or you can wait. You can file a claim at your full retirement age. I go into details about Social Security in Part III.

False Financial Finish Lines

Social security creates a false finish line for many. But the popularity of early claims can be a big problem – especially as you age. Maybe the program needs to make it easier to wait. In some ways, it was the birth of the retirement concept. But another dilemma of retirement is quality healthcare. You may live longer than you think. We are living longer. Yet many still want to retire as soon as social security benefits can start.

Here are some concepts to get the point across. Say you're shopping for a TV because your old one hit the fritz. The new tv is $600. It's the holidays, and you did your homework. You know $600 is a good deal. The store selling you the TV says you can buy it today for $600. But they're running low. Would you be willing to wait 6-8 weeks? They'll give you 8% (and 8% is the most they can offer you) off today's price and call you when the same TV is available, again.

Don't rationalize the question or your answer. It's not complicated. The TV is there today. You were there first. It's the best price in town. Is it worth you waiting 6-8 weeks for a lousy 8%?

This story shares something called opportunity cost. What could you do with the money in the meantime? Will that 8% savings make up for your lost TV time during the holidays?

I used 8% on purpose because 8% happens to be the 12-month increase retirees can realize by delaying a claim. And it's an increase on a lifetime check. It's not a one-time TV purchase.

But a social security check is a social security check that you've earned, you say. But 8% is 8%. Consider your circumstances and be mindful of what the numbers tell you. Maybe we're both right.

The trouble is that saving for retirement is self-controlled. And those who could benefit most from waiting tend not to wait. These are savers who have failed to save enough on their own. They are eager to claim benefits that are certain and predetermined for them. Even if this means their social benefits will provide less income for the rest of their life. Again, there's more about this in Part III.

What about this? Let's say you are flying home from a business trip. It's Friday afternoon. Your flight is late. Then it's overbooked. The airline is taking "volunteers" to take the next flight out. This means you may leave late tonight or even tomorrow morning. How much money would you need from the airline to delay your return home?

We value our time and the things we can do with that time. Airlines and retail have figured this out. You may be wise to apply this to your social security benefit, too.

Retirement as a Transition

Consider a transition into retirement. It can provide time to make the mental shift. But it can also help you save more.

Work three more years. But live with intent. Reward yourself by scheduling three or four long vacations during this time. Permit yourself time to transition.

You may not have enough money saved. If you are honest, it may be a leap of faith to retire and expect that you are financially prepared. Don't put the retirement cart in front of the horse. Your assets will be pulling for you the rest of your life. Are you set? A transition may be an excellent way of encouraging folks to stick to their savings habits for a few more years.

There is no magical age or number that retirement begins to appear. So make a personal retirement plan. Take your time. Then go.

I have yet to hear a client tell me that they wish they'd saved less for retirement.

If you can retire at 50, what a blessing. Even at 60 and 65, it is a blessing to retire in good health and with confidence that your assets can provide for you.

Maybe instead of submitted your resignation letter, you start to arrange extended vacations. Maybe you are lucky and can arrange to take unpaid leave.

A transition can be a time to balance your passions and redefine yourself. As I said at the beginning of this chapter, begin to shape your retirement with intent.

Go beyond the quick and easy answers. Explore what fulfills you. Perhaps you have a desire to be a photographer. Life had other priorities - until now. Now you can spend three hours at the county park taking photos of birds. Could you mentor other business owners? You could consult and take on odd jobs. You could see if a part-time teaching position is open in your college community.

Sure you might feel like you're done working. But if you are 65 and retired, what will you do for 20, 30, or 40 more years?

There's another question for retirees to think about. You may not have thought about your later years. Where will you live? Will you move closer to your family?

False Financial Finish Lines

Active retirees volunteer, spend time with family, travel, and do the things they enjoy.

In your 80's, 90's and 100's, you may not be as active. Going to the grocery store may be something that takes a great deal of organization and effort.

Regardless of where you are on your retirement journey, think about these things and more. Retirement is a false finish line.

You know this already. You keep giving and receiving in retirement.

The music of life doesn't dial down because you turn a certain age. Retirement is a blessing. Everything you love can have your undivided attention. You have much to teach the next generation. You have stories to share amongst your peers. Give it time. Let the retired life soak in. After all, transitions take time.

What's your retirement order?

Investments can serve as a means to life goals.

When we focus on you, rather than the numbers, profound things in your life can happen over time.

Lifestyle wealth planning is about bringing out the value of a dollar in your eyes. That's what money is for. It's the exchange of government notes for something you want more than notes.

I think of the parable of the lamp underneath the basket. What good does a lamp do you when you hide it under a basket? You need to lift the basket off, and then the light can show you the room and the world around you.

So have a look around before retirement. There's much to explore. There is no magical age that retirement begins to

False Financial Finish Lines

appear. You may think about it during bad weeks at work. You may think about it more and more as your friends talk about it in more earnest. Then friends may begin to retire and where will you be?

What's going to guide you? Numbers?

Or the world around you?

Family

Let's begin with home.

A family has all sorts of depth and love.

I come from a family of 11 children and two committed and loving parents. I'm the third oldest. We are lucky.

I have seen the challenge of balancing priorities with one and two incomes. I saw Mom buying 10-gallons of milk at a time. She once graduated to a commercial-sized milk bladder dispenser. We grew up in a home where we had two homemade bunk beds in one bedroom. The other bedrooms all had at least two beds.

Hand-me-down clothes were always in style. Memories came in the form of two week-long summer vacations. And who knows how Mom and Dad got us to behave in church? I can recall one time when Mom hurried to the back of the church with one of us in the midst of a full-blown tantrum. Okay…there was more than one tantrum at church.

If you peeked through the Mullin window, I'm sure you would feel love. Dinner was always on the table. Mom or Dad made dinner somewhere between work, sick kids, homework and helping us grow up. They did this while providing persistent encouragement and enriching experiences. They did this in the hopes that we may one day have a better life because of them.

False Financial Finish Lines

It was evident that my parent's priority was, and still is family.

I write about my parent's because it's another way that I can praise their efforts. And their accomplishments.

Life was good growing up. And we never missed a thing.

Growing up in a large family is a lot of fun. Our Christmas Eve seafood dinner is packed with energy and joy. We are never short of friends.

Parenting is the toughest job around. And I do think children can grow up to appreciate the love that raising any size family takes.

We were home for dinner the other night. We live a quick drive down the interstate from my parents. My dad sent an e-mail in the morning to the family, inviting us for dinner. Obviously, the family from the East Coast wouldn't be in attendance that evening. But they nonetheless received the same last-minute dinner invite.

My wife and I didn't reply until mid-afternoon. Finally, we decided we'd make our way down the interstate. We arrived 10-minutes before dinner. Our little man handed our host gifts to grandpa. My dad poured some great wine. Then we picked up conversation around the kitchen island. It looked like about four or five of my siblings would make it for dinner.

Mid-conversation, my dad, abruptly turned and headed outside without excusing himself. We made our way to my parents' retirement room. It's this pine wood, northern Minnesota themed room with a gas cast-iron fireplace as a focal point. Seconds later the old dinner triangle clanged. I laughed.

False Financial Finish Lines

Here is some background to this triangle bell. The triangle came from his parents' old farm. It's how they announced dinner at the farm. The bell called the children for dinner from the barn, fields, and sled hill. You could hear the bell on the farm no matter what farm chores. And so the bell rang now. We were just chatting with the man. I was pretty sure no children were out in the yard or at the park to hear the dinner triangle clang. But I could imagine the nostalgia my Dad got from ringing that dinner triangle.

Some of our happiest moments take place with our family surrounding us. Think of the weddings, holidays, and newborn children. The support of our family can alleviate some of our darkest days.

When I think about home, I think of our relationships and how many different passions exist. A family has depth. I think of the passage: "For where your treasure is, there will your heart be also." (Matthew 6: 21)

It's evident to me how our family deserves our love and energy.

Family can draw us away from the discipline of caring for our future selves financially.

It's difficult for me to write a book about financial finish lines and not address the dynamics of a family. It is a prominent place of tug-of-war at the family bank.

We'll save more when the kids finish school…

When the kids are married…

We'll be able to move when…

Our kids don't deserve to be in debt…

Headlines today talk about parents helping their kids out with their student loans. Some families have children who are spendthrifts. Some parents try to keep their children on course to graduate high school. Some parents boast about their young adult child's accomplishments, too.

Being a parent is the toughest job there is. And you're supposed to think about retirement between the hours of 5 a.m. and midnight, too?

Family and finance have depth. Money can quickly get entangled with emotions that we aren't prepared for or aren't ready or willing to address.

So what are you to do?

Get on the same page and identify what it is you are worried about or thinking about. What are your financial priorities? What should go first?

Have a meaningful conversation with those involved.

I'm not only talking about normal disagreements between husband and wife. I'm talking about a greater depth of family finance. We live in a world where senior parents don't tell their children that they can't afford prescriptions. Or that they can't afford to support their adult children any longer. There are those who need more care due to mental health issues and addiction. There are aging grandparents who may need care and attention but don't want to be a burden.

I'm talking about the tough stuff.

Family relationships have considerable complexity. So strive to have conversations about money that stay on point.

Money is money; it's numbers. If you have a significant other, then you ought to set aside time once a month to discuss your money. It may feel awkward at first. Start with the state of your family bank account. Discuss your income, debt and monthly expenses. Start by talking about the small stuff that arises. My wife and I may or may not disagree about buying premium gasoline, for instance. Talk about the small stuff. It's a good habit to develop so that the tough stuff doesn't feel so tough to talk about.

Then begin to address goals that you have. You may start to feel progress and control over your financial choices.

You may be surprised to learn how your spouse or significant other views the family bank account. Have this conversation before marriage. Have this conversation as you grow your family. Invite your children to join in as they get older.

Family and finance have serious depth. Stay on point.

When family stuff and challenges come up, talk it out. How does seeing your parents or grandparents age make you feel? What concerns do they have? Are there things you do not want to do when you are their age?

As a family grows through the depth continues to build.

Weddings are a massive undertaking for couples today. Others go against the grain and keep weddings simple.

As a parent, I can't imagine anything but the best for our little champion.

Acknowledge that whole left brain/right brain thing. It's that idea that says we make emotional and logical choices. With a family, this is no different.

It is challenging to separate how our gut wants to respond, versus how our brain tells us to respond. Our mind is playing tug-of-war with our heart.

Talk it out. What will help the family? Embrace conversations with your family.

False Financial Finish Lines

It may just be that your family is the most important thing to you. As you keep reading, you will notice life events and moments where your family and life story fit in.

Education: Helping Your Ducklings Cross the Road

I remember celebrating 100 days of school in kindergarten. What a milestone! We wore cool construction paper glasses shaped into the number "100". Then we counted how many days we had until school was out for the summer.

I remember gathering around the living room in the years that followed with my mom and siblings. My mom had received all our school supplies lists. It was particularly significant to get a new backpack. My mom would pass out crayons, scissors, pencils, paint, etc.

As our school supplies quartermaster passed items to us, she crossed the things off the list. Mission accomplished.

Our school system is full of finish lines. It embraces a child's attention span. It's seasonal. And there's always another mile marker to reach. You have one week of lessons, two quizzes, followed by a test on Tuesday the following week. These days grades are available on demand. Then you have Christmas break. Then there's the spring slide until the end of the year. A student sees assignments, reading material, quizzes, and tests throughout the year.

You learn to get past a finish line from an early age. Then you move on to the next topic, the next test, and the next year.

False Financial Finish Lines

Remarkably, many children learn to love topics, music and extracurricular activities.

When children choose to go to college, they will see a similar structure. Except at this point, it is a more mature process. It is self-controlled to some degree. You elect your own major. You then select which courses you'll take to fulfill graduation requirements. Colleges can be ecosystems for young adults. It is one of societies transitions to a life of independence.

If college is a transition, then why do adult children move back home after college? This return home is the boomerang effect. Young adults go to college. They become equipped to handle jobs and life. But young adults go home. What happens?

Children (young adults) often move home. According to Pew Research Center, in 2014, about 1 of 3 children ages 18-34 lived with their parents. It hadn't been like this in the US since the era right after the Great Depression. So something must have happened to cause this.

Some sociologists would name the recent recession of 2008-09 as the culprit. Others might say it is due to higher levels of student debt.

Regardless, I see it affect aspiring (would-be) retirees.

Some costs go along with housing a young adult. We love our children. We want them to grow up, yes. But we want them to be comfortable. Many parents are quick to assist their children but neglect their retirement funds. And we would fit right in if our little one ever needed help.

Growing up

By the age of about 22, many college graduates walk away with their diploma and a job on the horizon.

Many grads face a blank canvas next.

Independence hit me after graduation; like my body hitting the ground after flying off a swing. I had the next five and ten years of my life planned out. What I found was that life changes, but the passion and grit and values stick with you.

There's a lesson. Excellent work ethic, passion, and values are worth passing along to our children.

College graduation is like the void after retirement. Or the void between jobs.

What happens next? Is it an all-star companies job to motivate young adults? Maybe; but probably not.

Life can be a motivator. Job changes and promotions are motivators. Other things like marriage and a family are motivators. A new home may motivate young adults. But the motivation may be muted directly after graduation. It gets lost in the transition.

It is the first time many young adults no longer have another test to pass, another grade to graduate. Their friends may move away. Or they become occupied with their careers. There aren't the typical educational mile markers.

There is the elephant in the room. College loans.

College expenses have increased at unconscionable rates over the past decade.

Let's say it is the government's fault. Let's blame the school system. Or you could have a conversation about what your family and children can control.

False Financial Finish Lines

Please be careful about how you approach the topic. Will you describe loans as an advantage or a disability? Why should a child and parents take on debt at all for college? Society regards a college education as an opportunity.

Your children may have student loans around for a decade or longer. Help them view it as a privilege during that time.

Involve your children in the financial aid conversation. Head nods do not count as conversation. Coach your children. Inform them; don't tell them. If you are not sure of the financial aid process, then sit down with those that are.

College graduation is where the rubber meets the road. Are young adults built for delayed gratification? Can they pay their bills? Do they know what independence takes? As a parent, you hope they recall the lessons learned before going to college. Are they equipped to stare down immediate wants for longterm needs?

Forget loan types and interest rates for a moment.

Have they learned responsibility? What have they done to acquire a work ethic?

Were they given a chance to fail?

As a parent, what conversations did you have before they went to college?

Maybe this new reality has something to do with the boomerang effect in young adults? The motivation and praise are not there for young adults like it was all the way through college.

So, once again, maybe our choices lead with the heart. Perhaps young adults return to the place where they received support and encouragement. They go home.

Careers

You're lucky if you have a career where you feel satisfied. Hold on to that perspective. Work is a means to an end for many.

Are you satisfied with your career? The next few chapters address that thing we do before retirement: Work.

Careers are infamous for false finish lines. *If only I could get that promotion…If only I could get a raise…If I just had a different job…If only I could find satisfaction. I can't wait for my next vacation!*

This chapter can be brief. There are only two results of your career that I'll share. First, it's your income. Income is one result of your work. I want to help you realize how income rich you are. Then, I'll talk a bit about your lifestyle outside of work.

Your career provides a paycheck. You'll read more about how you tend to spend what you make — or more.

Realize how valuable your income is.

If you work for 40 years and make around $80,000, well, that's $3.2 million! So where does it all go?

Ah, yes, life. It has its ways of surprising us. Have you ever thought about how much you will make during your lifetime? The Social Security Administration takes your income into account. Your average salary helps determine your benefit. Maybe you take stock of your lifetime income, too.

Try prioritizing your life by voting with your dollars. Your earning potential can work in your favor if you catch on to this mindset earlier, rather than later.

You will have conflicting priorities. You have to pay your debts. You may have a family to raise. And retirement is so far off. You can save for retirement later.

How would you behave if you had 20 things to do at home this upcoming weekend before you leave for vacation? You'd probably tackle the 20 tasks with grace and zeal. The windows would get washed in a hurry. You would weed the garden. You'd make sure to change your business e-mail to an away message.

The thing is that once you plot out a retirement date on the long-term calendar, you know that it's approaching. You can't stop time. So focus on how much time you have left. Then realize what income and investments you have to work with. And take action.

Saving something rather than nothing is a good start.

Think about it like this: A little planning today could save you from a lot of work tomorrow. If you are not saving for retirement, what you're really saying is that you don't mind working longer. And maybe you don't.

If you are close to retirement, then rethink your lifestyle and priorities – now!

Life can be full of surprises. Careers can provide immense satisfaction and its share of stress. Financial priorities are a balancing act.

So, prioritize your personal life and career. Take a vacation. Use your available paid time off - don't bank it for next year. (Unless you have a super relaxed vacation planned for next year that will need more days off.)

The grind is real. Life is short.

So focus on where your income is going. Spend some time thinking about future you so that one day you can potentially have what you want when you want it.

That's pretty much all I need to say about careers.

Take stock of your lifetime income potential. Balance your life and career. Save something, rather than nothing for retirement.

You may be glad you did.

The Home You Make

"A man travels the world over in search of what he needs and returns home to find it." -George A. Moore, *Irish Writer*

Abraham Lincoln grew up in a log cabin. And do you know how big that cabin likely was? It was probably the size of your living room. According to the National Park Service, it was likely 16x18 feet. They had no carpet. The cabin had dirt floors and one window. Could you imagine a family of 4 or 8 sleeping in this arrangement? (National Park Service, Abraham Lincoln Birthplace, online)

Today homes are much more significant. Home seems to be a place where we want as much (or more) comfort as we can afford. We want a community with a good school district. We want reasonable taxes. We want parks. We want good neighbors that won't mow the lawn at 6 a.m. on Saturday.

It seems like folks are moving more often than before. Job changes have something to do with this. But what about neighbors who move 1-mile away? My parents have lived in their existing home for more than 20-years. Of course, with 11 children, they had to do a little remodeling.

Home is home. The idea of home has not changed since the Century log cabins in Kentucky. Where do you live? Usually, people search for a home because of economic and life choices. A job may cause someone to move. You may wish to send your children to a different school district. You may want to move closer to (or further from) your family.

Home should be a place to live, first. It's a need that dates back to the caveman. (They lived in caves.) So the adage that folks tend to raise their living standards to or above what they earn comes to mind. Home is also a financial decision.

You very well may start your search with an online calculator. Many searches begin on home search sites. You know, search first, and figure out how you can afford it later? Or you could be different and learn about how much money you should spend on your home.

But phony finish lines can appear in home prices, mortgages and dream homes, too. Learn about good financial choices before you buy a house. A home purchase can be a huge moment in your life. Think this through before you start to search.

A home search should begin with a financial professional. A professional that understands that life can change. It doesn't happen this way the majority of the time. But it should.

I'm sharing some personal insights about your home from a particular financial lens. Consult your home professionals and bank or mortgage broker with specific questions.

First, a home has a way of surprising you with expenses. Know that unexpected expenses in life will always exist. Every year you'll have an expected unexpected something that you'll need to cover. So save some dough before you buy a home.

You should learn about the idea behind debt-to-income ratios and ask questions. Ratios are a lender's formula for figuring out how big of a monthly payment they might be comfortable with for you. There usually is a conservative ratio, moderate ratio, and a maximum ratio.

Don't begin a home search in a backwards manner by searching for homes online. Before you know it you will decide granite countertops are essential. You begin to imagine your family playing in the backyard. Then you "heart" them or "like" them and save them in your online search, right? Then you start your showings. You may look at 10 or 20 homes in-person.

During your search, you or your realtor may suggest looking at a home outside your comfort zone. But it's great. It fits a lot of the homes that you "hearted" online.

Suddenly, nothing but this standard meets your needs.

Let the rationalization begin.

It's a little on the high side of what we are comfortable buying. But our income is only going to go up. If we bought a "cheaper" home, then we'd probably move in a couple of years anyway, right? Those upgrades are just so lovely...and we'd have to spend a lot of money to make those upgrades ourselves, and I'll get a bonus this year anyway. We're going to spend so much time in that kitchen...

Honey, I want this one!

Don't rationalize a purchase like your home. Take your time to appreciate what the tedious and annoying math is telling you.

Try one conservative approach to calculating your home mortgage payment. What do you earn in a year? What do you keep after you have funded retirement and pay taxes? If you make $80,000 and pay about $10,000 in taxes, then you have about $70,000 to spend during the year. You probably have at

False Financial Finish Lines

least one car payment. And you should save money for retirement. You may learn you could "afford" a $1750-2650 house payment. (This should include insurance and tax payments.) But you may be more fit with a $700-2000 house payment. That's a conservative approach to home payment math.

Think about what could happen if life changes suddenly. We tend to think of the future more optimistically. And yet our past teaches us hard life lessons. Why is that?

What could happen? Maybe you're laid off. Perhaps a loved one gets sick, and you want to move closer to them suddenly. It is possible that a significant expense comes up. (And it's always something.)

Approach your home purchase conservatively. You might be more comfortable when the somethings of life arise.

Home prices are out of your control. Let me tell you something: Home prices rise and fall. Up and down cycles usually transform over the years. Sometimes prices can fall, and you need to move.

Yet homes are pronounced as an investment. Robert Shiller, a Nobel Prize Laurette, talks about home valuations. Home prices go up and down in shorter cycles. In his book, *Animal Spirits* (2009), he says home prices average out over more extended periods of time. He considers various factors. He also explains how existing home prices over long periods of time tend to follow an average line. That average home price line? It declines.

False Financial Finish Lines

Home improvement costs and new neighborhoods have something to do with this. Neighborhoods and homes seem to move in cycles like so much else in life and money.

Home cycles are essential to recognize. If you look at what happened up until mid-2008, you'll see that home prices were rising above average. They were way above the average. This increasing trend is the type of period where it likely paid to be a conservative buyer and stick to life needs.

You might hear the word "investment" quite a lot during a home search.

Your home is a place to live.

Here's the definition of "investment" from Merriam: "the action or process of investing money for profit or material result."

Could you read that, again? Please.

If you live in your home for the long-haul and make the repairs you ought to make, and the home ages ... could you read the definition of, "investment," to me, again? Now tell me that your home is an investment.

Fine. It's an investment. It's an investment that could need a good deal of tender-loving care. It's an investment that will see spikes in value and decreases in value – if you stay put long enough to see it. You will replace various things like carpet and appliances.

In 2006, if you bought a home as an "investment," you may have felt a world of hurt. Especially if you believed you could sell in the next few years for a profit. Let me share your fairytale ending. You lost. Your investment tanked. You were under water. If you had to move and you recently moved in, then you had problems. Now if you bought and you were planning on staying...that's a different story.

A home is a place where you live, first. Here's Merriam's definition of "home": "the place where one lives permanently, especially as a member of a family or household."

You saw that word "permanently," right?

It seems like a lot more folks get burned when they are motivated to think outside the financially stable – and I believe – prudent box.

That's all.

Then there are big influencer's that proclaim the need to be financially responsible. Famous personalities get folks attention. Frankly, I think material that motivates people to pay attention to their money with more care is a good thing.

But you have to be careful with blanket statements. Some choices depend on your circumstances. Sometimes this loud advice spills into the mortgage payment arena. Should you hurry up and pay off a mortgage? That depends on your circumstances.

The Millionaire Next Door (Stanley and Danko, 1996), looked at the home purchases of your "average" millionaire. In 1996, the authors found that many of these folks who lived reasonable and average lives had paid off their home mortgage. But they also saw that the home value didn't necessarily rise with the owners net worth. Meaning, that it didn't matter if a millionaire had one or 5 million. They still lived in reasonably sized homes.

You can read the book. It's a good read. The homes were not mansions. They weren't starter homes either. They were

False Financial Finish Lines

reasonable when you compared what these homeowners had amassed in wealth.

Well, William Danko died. And Thomas Stanley authored a book more than a decade after their co-authored book. His book, "Stop Acting Rich," sounded the drum of misbehavior. Again, he emphasized that a home is a place to live. So, why did so many folks own large, expensive homes? Someone with a high income occupied these charming homes. A high salary does not equal high net worth. You can quickly spend your income. Finally, Stanley addresses something that I haven't talked about…yet. That's peer pressure. (Stanley, 2006.)

Do you want to know about financial peer pressure? You don't believe you fall for it? It takes great self-control not to.

You know about the Saturday lawn mowing phenomena? That first zealous neighbor gets their lawn mower out early in the morning. You are still reading the newspaper. Then 40-minutes later you hear another lawn mower. Before you know it you're out mid-afternoon mowing your lawn. The lawn needs to be mowed. Still, there's nothing like a nudge from neighbors.

That's peer pressure!

The same thing happens with money. One neighbor buys a new car, a wreath for their door, or a bounce house for a party. Before you know it the other neighbors have wreaths, upgraded cars, and bounce houses.

False finish lines appear a great deal with homes.

You just moved into a home you love.

Now you want to finish your basement. You want to build a porch or a deck. You want granite countertops. You want a new car…

False Financial Finish Lines

The furniture doesn't match your style anymore... If you could only have a home with some privacy, a fence, a dog, a different school system, or 40 acres with a stream running through it.

I'm not knocking wreaths. But you'll probably notice the difference in your neighbors' bank accounts, too (Stanley, 2006). Everyone in the neighborhood has a different income. And it's not yours.

What happens after you get these things? Maybe one day you will have these things. But take your time. Your bank account and future self will thank you.

Home After Retirement

It just seems to me that those that retire without a mortgage payment seem to be much more comfortable. And why shouldn't they be? They are free from a very common budget expense. If you're looking for a section of this chapter to take away or highlight, this fact is it.

You can retire with a mortgage. For many, this will be the reality. So examine your lifestyle. Examine where the money goes. Then revisit where you live and what your expectations are.

Maybe you'll be one of the many who is a part-time retiree? Perhaps you'll sell your home so you can move to an association where the lawn is taken care of for you?

And don't mind that wreath. I think it brightens your home, too!

Entrepreneurs: The Independent Path

If you know an entrepreneur, then you've seen the look in their eyes on a Saturday afternoon outing. They are with you, but the gears in their brain are churning.

This chapter may appeal to you if you're an entrepreneur, or if you've ever had an idea that you thought you'd like to undertake.

The Beginning

How does one become an entrepreneur?

Entrepreneurs are usually born from some pain point. I've seen many businesses develop because a budding entrepreneur didn't like what was happening at their current employer. That individual had the motivation to create a business for their livelihood. The entrepreneur also happened to be right in a niche.

Entrepreneurs also may develop out of an idea. They don't like the idea of having to do something one way and expending all this time and money. So they create a widget as a solution. Then out of this widget is born a process. From this process, a business can be born.

I know entrepreneurs who did go to business school and got some form of Master's degree. They are in the minority.

False Financial Finish Lines

The majority may happen to have a degree of some kind. But I'll suggest that the pain point and passion is what drives them.

A pain point pushes you to the point to take the financial risk. You are going to give up rich corporate benefits. You are going to give up a generally reliable paycheck. You will be in charge of daily operations. You will find the help you need. You will keep inventory and review what you sell for quality. You will also be in charge of your brand and promotion. Then you will be in charge of your service and operations. Does this sound like a lot? Because there's more.

Many entrepreneurs are entrepreneurs by necessity and sort of without knowing it. They are aware of it on some level, but they do not place themselves in the category of an entrepreneur. A plumber has expertise in their field. They may have their last name on the truck they drive around. But at the end of the day, they go home and spend time with their family. The business blends well with their life routines.

An exciting thing about developing a business is realizing you have a real chance of keeping it in the family. Or selling it.

Family owned business often gets passed on to children because they grew up helping mom and dad. Usually, the children would help with the day-to-day chores. It is indeed a family business.

Then what about the reward of selling your business to someone else? There is a reason that business is a part of the American Dream. It began with trades in Europe. It started with trades in Asia and Africa. It was brought to the United States by pilgrims and travelers. It is a part of our world.

A farmer is the quintessential example of an entrepreneur. They make a living off the land. They use technology and science to develop their crop and livestock. They hire helping hands. They rarely take a vacation.

Every year a farmer battles the elements. They rely on the harmony of nature. At the end of each cycle of their business, they hope to turn a profit. They strive to limit their losses. They work before the sun comes up and work past sundown. They are masters of their work.

They have to have a passion for what they do. Many farmers have family that has farmed or still farm. But they must have a desire for continuing the family farm. Why else would you get up every day and labor for 12+ hours throughout the year? There are other ways to make money.

The cycle of the farming business can reap good financial rewards. Many years are tough.

So, just for fun, the next time you buy sweet corn, go ahead and give a farmer you know a call. Ask them how sweet corn grows. You could do the same for the farmer who raises cattle. The next time you enjoy a burger, go ahead and ask your farmer friend about his herd. Ask him what some of the cows' names are.

Farming is a tradition for many. It is an evolving tradition. It is why so many farmers get together throughout the year. They are just like any entrepreneur. They want business to last through business cycles and droughts. If they're fortunate enough they may pass the farm on to another generation.

What's in it for you?

What are the benefits of farming? Why do entrepreneurs tune out the world around them and commit themselves to their work?

False Financial Finish Lines

A lot likely has to do with personality. The ultimate reward is that you're in charge. Just like a farmer, there is immense satisfaction in growing something yourself.

If you're a hobby gardener, then you already understand. There are stages of gardening. You have daily, weekly, and annual chores. At the end of every day, you can stand back and admire your garden.

There are benefits to being in business for yourself. They are regularly changing. So it's probably best to put professionals in your corner to guide you.

According to, The Millionaire Next Door, a book by Thomas Stanley and William Danko, a millionaire is more likely to be self-employed and self-made. So, you have the millionaire club to strive for.

I think that the ability to create wealth is likely due to good habits and an appreciation for risk. Entrepreneurs have to take on a certain amount of risk. The risk may be understated in your mind. Entrepreneurs sometimes wear blinders. Muting the risk down in your mind helps you approach risk differently. But I have heard spouses of entrepreneurs describe the transition from a stable career to self-employment as "scary" at first.

A farmer doesn't take the time to think too often about doing anything else. Just like a dentist with a private practice doesn't think about really doing anything else. It is their niche. But there is a risk. There is also a great deal of stress.

This trade-off between risk and reward is most evident during stressful periods.

False Financial Finish Lines

A Rewarding Life Ignored

An entrepreneur's mind is often churning. It's probably best to develop and nurture a hobby or several hobbies outside of your niche work for that reason. Sure, entrepreneurs wonder about all sorts of other things they could be doing. But it's always the passion that brings us back.

Discipline is something I don't know how to teach. It's something that I think I have though. Some call it grit.

Grit involves you visualizing the finish line. Then you pass the finish line with passion while hardly acknowledging the finish. An entrepreneur is never truly satisfied. Are you? There are daily, weekly, monthly, and annual things you'd like to try. You can continuously develop and learn something new.

A farmer may consider winter an "offseason." This means that the farmer has a chicken barn or dairy barn or machinery that they only spend a total of 7-10 hours a day on.

An entrepreneur can be a great accumulator of wealth. Traits like discipline and a never-settle attitude can help their wealth develop.

Self-Employed Finish Lines

Who says a farmer needs to be done farming at 75-years-old? Who says a widget seller can't keep selling at 80?

Passion and a never-settle attitude keep these folks moving ahead. Sure they follow the breadcrumbs along the way. If they do stop it's usually intentional and planned. Other times – more often than you'd think – it's unplanned and unrehearsed. And this is important: This is what can cause real problems.

Health and life eventually catch-up with all of us. Entrepreneurs may develop a high tolerance for risk and pain. We also like to tune out distractions so we can focus. Once in a while, it's wise to plan for a transition. It's useful to visualize the future without you at the steering wheel of your business.

Remember, a pain point may have pushed you into your passion or perhaps you grew up learning it from your family. Eventually, you'll either want to or have to transition away from what you do.

When do you win? When's your last harvest season? When is enough, enough?

If planning retirement in advance is smart, then surely this can apply to your business exit, right?

Good business operators know that their time must come to an end. This is easier for professionals and business owners who hang around like-minded friends and colleagues. They know that their time is approaching to pass the baton on to the next generation. Good things must come to an end. That's the way it's always been.

There will be tests of this transition and missteps. Maybe a business or practice has been family owned and operated. Now choices need to be made about the businesses legacy. Will it continue with other family members, close, or transition outside the family? These are all intensely personal choices.

Announce Your Retirement

There are no victory laps for entrepreneurs. There are only pursuits and achievements. You can step back once in a while and appreciate what you've achieved and obtained. But there's no sign for you that says, "Exit Ahead."

False Financial Finish Lines

Have you been looking for an Exit Ahead sign? Your family and customers have perhaps been wondering the same. What will you tell them? An exit for an entrepreneur is challenging. One reason for this is the lifestyle. Self-employment is a lifestyle. Much of the style is being busy. Your life blends in with your work. It is no different for your money.

The self-employed have a unique view of money. You pay yourself. You are acutely aware of the income taxes that get paid. The money you keep after tax goes to fuel your business and hopefully yourself. If you told me it feels like there is a tug-of-war occurring with your money, it would not surprise me.

I think of business owners finances like your lungs. We need lungs to breathe and live. You need money to fuel your business and life. For much of our self-employed lives, we breathe with two interconnected lungs. We have a right lung and a left lung. Your right lung holds your business income, assets, and expenses. Your left lung holds your personal income, assets, and debts. But your two lungs breathe together. One can affect the other. And this connection between the two is what can make transitioning difficult. The choices we make with money sometimes blurs the division between the two lungs.

Of course, you want to do what's best for your business. You would also like to make a good living. Sometimes you need a nudge from others to think about your finances.

How do you capture and reshape the value and accomplishment that your business lung has breathed into your life? How do you reposition your wealth to shape the next phase in life? How do you retrain your business lung to breathe more like your personal lung as you move on?

Don't wait for a pain point to push you out. That's not like you. Take control of what you're doing today by thinking ahead. Make a plan to shape your life outside of business. Then work the transition plan. Working the plan is what you are good at. Then carry on.

A Physician's Journey

I get to dedicate this chapter to the world's most wonderful wife.

My wife is a physician.

It seems she already has a treasure chest of gratitude from her patients. I'm glad; for she has poured half her life into pursuing her career.

She is still the only individual I know that is doing what she said she wanted to do "when she grew up." She wrote a brief essay in high school about practicing podiatry. Moreover, she is living her goal today. Of course, I know her priorities are family and relaxation.

I like to share that she has appointed herself the guardian of all animals. She has such love for all living things.

And this is what makes you so incredible and kind.

I love you, Becky.

The pursuit of advanced professions crosses many false finish lines.

Your first step begins in high school. A physician likely needs to stand out in their class to get accepted to an undergraduate school. Then they probably need to stand out in a 4-year undergraduate school. So don't forget to study. Every semester you will take courses that are inside a science building, which half the student population avoids.

(I would bypass this building on campus every time I could. I enjoy science. But my knowledge ends at knowing where my arms and knees are. My son knows that stuff.)

You'll stay up late. You'll buy very expensive, and heavy books. You'll take classes where half the students drop out after the first test. You'll probably have to settle for at least one "C."

Then you will graduate!

Celebrate your graduation. Enjoy the tears, smiles, hugs, and handshakes at your commencement ceremony. It is a strange time when you are pursuing an advanced profession. You know you have more education in front of you. Another ten years may pass. Your friends from college may have ten years of a career underneath them already.

Before you graduate from college, you will have taken the MCAT test. (A test for seriously smart people like yourself.) Or maybe you'll have a year or ten off and try your hand in the workforce. Eventually, you'll take your entry exams and apply to medical school.

Medical School

Medical school is full of lines to cross and stuff to study. The fun stuff comes when you work on cadavers and real live patients in clinic settings. Then it's onward to about a year of rotations. Rotations entail a whirlwind of changes. Least of which is finding a place to sleep. You may crash in hotels, apartments, or friends couches. If you're lucky, you may find a well-funded hospital program who has quarters for folks like you!

False Financial Finish Lines

Have you ever dreaded an interview in your life? Or maybe you got nervous before a date? Imagine that this interview is going to last 30-days. Then you have 10-12 of these such interviews in a row. This is what your rotation year might feel like. Bring your antiperspirant.

So the journey carries on. You finish your rotations. Now it is time for you to list your favorite rotation, and then list your second, and third, etc. Meanwhile, the programs you visited for 30-days will determine if they want you or not. That's right. You weren't the only one attending their program. Others are hoping to work as an indentured servant for at least 2-3 years, too.

By the way, you have to be confident that the program you list as #1 wants you, too. If they don't, then you'll go to your #2. But if your #2 choice doesn't want you, then you'll go to your #3. So you have to be confident that your #1 choice is going to want you. It's the most archaic system I've seen. Oh, but it's not proper etiquette to ask your 30-day interviewer (rotation/hospital) if they do want you. So it's like dating somebody for a month and then not hearing from them, again. What did they think of you?

It feels a lot like this scene from The Giver by Lois Lowry. The children are assigned to different areas of their community to work – for life. It doesn't matter what the child thinks. It matters where the Elders believe they are best suited.

If you've seen draft days in professional sports, then you may have an idea of what it's like. It's probably the most archaic human lottery system that I can think of. And remember, you're not negotiating a multi-million dollar contract like a professional athlete. You're hoping to match with a program that you NEED to further your education.

Oh no, you don't get to practice with the public until you've completed a residency.

So, Match Day arrives.

You match with a residency program. Maybe it wasn't your #1. Perhaps it was #5. Still, another finish line crossed – hooray! Hopefully, your worn moving boxes are strong enough to endure one more move. You're going to your residency program!

You'll have many more finish lines to cross. You'll make friends. You'll cry. You'll celebrate every year as your senior residents graduate from their residency. Their graduation gives you hope; that will be you one day.

Meanwhile... Your Finances and Loan Statements

During your journey, you will be combating compounding interest. Well, you will try to tackle it. You will be the poster for 'delayed gratification.' Maybe you will delay fun toys a decade longer while you dig out of loans.

By the time you're a resident, most of your friends will have had years of salary and promotions behind them.

You are different. Your residency program includes a set salary. And it is none too generous.

You can secure a higher income in time. Meanwhile, that backpack filled with six-figure debt bricks is getting heavy.

Keep the Faith

There is a scale for wealth. For decades, as an aspiring physician, you'll remain on one side. But soon the scale and its momentum will tip.

False Financial Finish Lines

I can explain. Do you remember the game, *Life*? Perhaps you have it in your game closet. In the game, you can choose to go to college, or you can elect to start off with your career. The advantage of starting with a job is you begin with zero loans.

The disadvantage is you only get one chance to pick a career. When you go to college, you will take on loans. But you will also get to choose from three different professions soon. Presumably, you have a higher chance of selecting a career that can give you a higher salary. Now, I'm sure *Life* is an accurate depiction of your life...

But I'm going to carry on by explaining the Scale of Wealth.

One side of the scale holds your income and assets like your savings and retirement. The other side of the scale holds your debts and bills.

Your first job can give you more freedom. You have money to spend. You have a few bills to pay. The Scale of Wealth is tipped in your favor.

Then you buy stuff like a college education, a car, and a home. You have children. You amass debt. The scale tips toward debt and bills.

The Scale of Wealth can remain balanced by paying debts on time or paying them off in full. It's normal to see the scale shift between debt and income a great deal during our working lives.

The trick is funding retirement while the scale tips back-and-forth. When our children grow up, and our careers advance, the Scale of Wealth seems to tip in our favor.

What do you do at this point with your money? Most of us should put it into retirement or pay down remaining debts.

False Financial Finish Lines

Again, the Scale of Wealth applies to healthcare professionals, too. The difference – and the difference is huge – is that you don't begin making a physician's salary right away. The scale is tipped against you for quite a while. You also get to drag a six-figure debt along for the ride.

Do you know how much interest alone can accrue on $200,000 in just one year? A lot. Imagine running a marathon with a 10-pound weight on your back. For a healthcare professional? That 10-pound weight is more like 100-pounds.

Would you prefer to run a marathon with 10-pounds on your back or 100?

The High-Income Earners Dilemma

In medical school, you take on this debt as a means to an end. The same goes for other career tracks, by the way.

So you'll balance your debts with improved income – someday soon. And you'll have a surprise there once your paychecks start arriving.

The physician's dilemma is a multi-pronged one. Once you start down the pathway of becoming a physician, you begin to add debt. Some solutions to shedding your loans are a higher than average income, a magical lottery ticket, or a sizable inheritance.

So short of having a wealthy aunt or winning the lottery, you feel the need to labor on. You need to pursue a job that can balance the Scale of Wealth in your favor.

So you march on because you genuinely feel a calling to ease pain and suffering in the world. And you have a Scale of Wealth that won't budge, to boot.

False Financial Finish Lines

After three years of medical school, one year of rotations, and another three to five years of residency, you are ready to work. You are a free agent in the physicians' marketplace.

The debt load shouldn't bother physicians-in-training – too much. It's a proud debt to carry. Many don't have the courage, discipline or smarts to choose this path – even if they wanted to.

Taxes and Balance

As I said, it's a multi-pronged dilemma for high-income earners. When a physician finds work, hopefully, they receive an above average salary in the community they choose to work.

Here's the act to balance after the paychecks start: loan interest and taxes. We'll get to life and retirement.

Loan interest and taxes seem to tilt the Scale of Wealth against you.

I already mentioned the average six-figure debt. Still, the highest bill a physician may incur at any point in their career is their tax bill.

So now the physician is paying sizable loans down and contributing to society in the form of higher taxes. This dilemma begins the first year she begins to serve the public!

It's a dilemma in wealth accumulation. Employer plans can add or subtract from this. Some employers offer retirement plans. But they may not allow newcomers to take part right away. This can be a problem. You'll see.

One voice says to be grateful you have taxes to pay. It means you have something others don't. But the rational and objective Scale of Wealth says you have bills to pay. You'd like to see the scale tip in your favor before you turn 70.

False Financial Finish Lines

The tax, income and debt dilemma should be discussed holistically with the retirement topic. Sorry. It feels complicated. But it's not *that* complicated.

Acknowledge one weight on the scale at a time. Take an inventory of your debt, taxes, and savings. Then focus on how the pieces shape your wealth over time. Remember, to make the scale move you need to take decisive steps over time. Right now when you remove $1,000 of income on the one side to pay $1,000 of debt on the other, your scale appears to improve marginally. All you did was take $1,000 that you earned and paid it toward something you owe.

Here is a gross analogy. I could eat a bag of chips and then workout enough to burn those calories. But that's not a balanced diet. And I'm not going to lose weight doing this. You're looking for longterm results. Paying off debt is good. Paying off debt while funding retirement is ideal.

How do all the pieces work in concert? How can we try to tip the scale with convincing long-term momentum?

Here's how a high-income earner can approach this:

•Save for Retirement and Keep Going: Max out your employer plan. Speak up if one isn't made available to you. Then seek to invest more in non-retirement accounts and your savings.

•Focus on Cash Flow: Seek a balance on your Scale of Wealth. If you could make $30 on every hundred you have or $6 on every hundred, which would you pursue? Undoubtedly, the $30, right? Well, what would you assume to do first? Pay off your student loans with a 6% rate on them? Or invest your money in a retirement plan that may yield you a deduction of $30 in taxes for every $100 saved?

•College Planning: As of 2018, the financial aid rules generally don't favor a family with a high income. Have this conversation early – like when your family is young. Like before you leave the hospital with your firstborn. (Kidding. Sort of.) This is because the parent's income is a significant factor. Are you likely to have a high salary when your children are in college? Plan for it. Other financial aid factors may include good grades and your child's extracurricular activities. Then you can pursue scholarships relentlessly. If suitable, consider using 529 College Savings accounts and other investment options.

Retirement

There's a well-worn path to becoming a physician. It's an impressive accomplishment. It's also a journey that has finish line after finish line...after finish line to cross.

Unfortunately, your retirement is something that you ought to become aware of and understand early on. Even in residency, you should grasp your options for paying off loans. How much of a priority should this be in your life? How will maxing out a retirement plan affect your taxes? Should you be investing in a non-retirement account?

Before you hurry to lavish yourself with rewards, please size up your retirement.

Comfort is in the eye of the beholder. And there is an old truth to the income you make: You often tend to spend what you make (or more). Define your definition of comfort.

False Financial Finish Lines

Recommit to this definition when spending your money. This is a critical habit of comfortable retirees.

Besides, a million bucks ain't worth a million bucks anymore. Think bigger.

Yes, physicians and high-income earners must realize early on what it will take to retire. Your numbers may surprise you. But the planning today can be worth it tomorrow. One day you may want to live off of your wealth for the rest of your life.

Wouldn't that be nice?

Measure Twice, Retire Once

"If you don't know where you are going, any road will get you there."
Lewis Carroll (Author of *Alice in Wonderland*)

That above Lewis Carroll quote sums up the reason for planning.

Right?

Think of retirement more holistically. It's numbers and details. But it is mind, body, and soul. Your money helps fund life experiences.

Living in retirement is best thought of as a transition. There is the pre-retirement phase that may be as long as ten years. It's crunch time. It's the time when you want to start focusing on high-priority, short-term goals.

A successful launch into retirement requires a few things. You'll pull on several income levers to fund your retirement. Your levers are your retirement portfolio, any pensions, and social security.

This income will take the place of your paycheck. It will determine how much money you have coming in – versus how much you expect to go out in a year.

False Financial Finish Lines

Relying on your retirement income sources can be emotional. You no longer have a steady paycheck to refill your bank account.

When you are saving for retirement, it is like you are filling up a big water balloon that continues to expand. When you retire, it's a different mindset. Now you're looking at this water balloon and wondering how do I move this thing without making it burst!? When you need to live off this money it's like you are poking a hole in the big water balloon. You let the water flow out. Retirement withdrawals are very much about the flow rate of money. You want to handle your money, so the balloon does not burst, and you're only left holding fragments of your nest egg.

There are reasonable fears that retirees and pre-retirees develop. These fears have to do with diminishing health, diminishing portfolio values, and unknowns. These fears tap into a fundamental concern of loss and control.

What's the antidote or ointment for retirement fears? You have your retirement plan. Then there is life and the actions you take to add or take from this plan. Plans change. So there's also strategy. A flexible strategy can adjust as retirement changes.

If a strategy is not enough to buy your confidence, then save more. Take action. Put off your transition to retirement. Many self-controlled solutions can help you ease retirement fears.

An Informed View

Funding your retirement lifestyle is a math problem. We complicate it with our fears. One emotional motivation for funding retirement is the fear of running out of money.

Fear can be like walking on a treadmill. You can hear me tell you 7-times to have confidence. But you keep walking on your treadmill...and never move on from the spot you are in today.

Would you retire today if you knew there was a chance that your retirement portfolio could turn to $0? Would you go skydiving if you knew there was a 10% chance that your parachute wouldn't open? How about a 40% chance? 2%?

Seek a balance between real data and trust. Then save more.

Again, two self-controlled solutions can help alleviate concerns. (1) Delay your full retirement; consider transitioning toward full retirement. (2) Save more.

Saving more can be helpful. Besides, retirees don't tell me that they wish they saved less for retirement.

A Fictitious-Utopian Retirement Life:
The Story of Joseph and Jane

All the habits that you've learned and practiced with your money have added up to this moment. Now it's time to look at the resources you have and ask how to spend them.

I'll share with you this example of a couple who transitioned into retirement. It is, of course, a wholly imagined circumstance and story. Names, characters, businesses, places, events, locales, and incidents are either the products of the author's imagination or used in a fictitious manner. Any resemblance to actual persons, living or dead, or actual events is purely coincidental.

The story of Joseph and Jane draws upon life events. It also calls on strong financial habits.

Joseph and Jane were doing well in their 50's. They finally had their children in or through college. They wanted to get a cabin home because they thought they might enjoy more time at the cabin during the weekends. Joseph was still working at his practice as a dentist. Jane was running a non-profit charity, which she enjoyed.

Joseph wanted to pay off their home. Jane wanted to pay off the kids college loans. Together they decided that they could do a little bit of each. They had made good money but now made more than they ever had before. Together they earned about $300,000. They were maxing out their company retirement plans. They still had extra money left over.

At this point in their life, they had become so used to living paycheck to paycheck. They didn't go on grand vacations. They were homebodies. So they invested extra money they had in a non-retirement account. This could give them another account to spend from in the future for various goals and expenses. They were also told to pay off their mortgage in the next 5-7 years. But they should not get too excited about paying it off earlier than that.

They enjoyed giving back to their community. They tithed 10% of their earned income to a few favorite charities including their church. But they now thought they might be behind on retirement savings. Together, with their professionals, they realized they were spending $90,000 a year. Less than what they thought because they were earning so much now.

It was important for Jane to keep track of their expenses.

Years went by. Joseph and Jane saw friends around them retiring. But what jarred Joseph at 62, was the death of a good friend. He kept telling Jane, "I know I'm fine. But his death kind of spooked me; woke me up. I've worked my whole life. Why do I keep working so much?"

This became some of their bullet-pointed strategy:

•Joseph transitioned his business to another dentist. Fortunately, there were still enough teeth in town that needed a dentist's care.

•Joseph started stepping back from his practice. He let his younger colleague take on more of the responsibilities.

•After five years, Joseph was only working 1-2 days a week. The rest of his time became consumed by work on their cabin, casual lunches with Jane, and life.

•Jane continued to help support and grow the non-profit she worked for. She didn't know if she wanted to be at work all of the time.

And how did they pay for this transition?

Again, it helped that they had good spending and saving habits. But the other thing that helped was Joseph's planned and calculated winding down of his business.

Joseph still had money coming in from his business. They continued to save for retirement and live on this money.

Jane kept working. Jane was not interested in retiring. She might retire when their first grandkids came along!

They decided to request social security when they turned 70. This was when they were ready to claim their benefits. They based this on many things. An important factor that they both considered was good health. In fact, both of Joe's parents were still living. Jane's mother was still living and lived nearby. So by the time they were 70, they were receiving social security retirement benefits. But they were not withdrawing money from their retirement assets.

They did not take a penny from their retirement portfolio until age 75.

So what if they hadn't paid off their home?

They may have been saving less for retirement. They could have retired still. But they would have been drawing money out of their retirement funds sooner.

What if they wanted to stop working sooner?

You mean if their son, Alexander, was older and he already had grandkids? Sure; they might begin living off of their retirement portfolio sooner. Withdrawing money from their retirement assets might help them delay social security. Delaying social security was a primary goal for Jane.

Joseph and Jane sound like they have a pretty healthy and above average life, right?

This on purpose, sorry. The fact is that life does change for us. We could pretend that Joseph and Jane had a significant health crisis in their late 40's and this set them back. We could pretend that they hadn't practiced the responsible habit of saving. We could pretend that they had corporate jobs and made a total of $90,000 together. The more change you experience on your walk toward retirement, the more complicated retiring can become.

The good news is retirement is relative. Income is relative. You tend to spend what you make. Unfortunately, many, many folks do not save what they should in comparison to what they make.

So, as dull and non-dramatic as the story of Joseph and Jane may be, it is told according to their life. They spend less than they earn. They wait for their social security benefits to increase. Importantly, they talk things through.

Your Retirement
Different events can influence us. That pain or fear can drive us to make significant choices. These choices can alter your retirement outlook. An ideal retirement from my point of view is one that is planned for decades and decades in advance.

Often, retirement is a lifestyle that you transition toward gracefully. It becomes the next natural step. You may be thinking, Okay that's great for you and others. But I'm 63 ... 65 ... 55 and nowhere near prepared.

Remember, it's all highly personal. It may be best to evaluate your lifestyle. Change what needs to be changed. You may have some things that you need to change that feel uncomfortable.

Perhaps you have some big expectations. I'm not telling you to consider these things. But you may have to look at the big line items like your home, boat, hobbies, etc. It's relative. It always is.

If it's any reassurance – and I'm sure it's not much – there are those who make great gobs of money and don't have nearly enough saved to sustain them. It's all relative.

Little habits and changes in our lives can make a big difference. Small adjustments today can add vast amounts of security to our life later.

The transition from earning a paycheck to retirement can be intimidating.

I'm trying to simplify something. Spending in retirement should feel familiar. What money will come into your bank account to spend? You're going to claim different benefits like social security and any pension you may have. You may draw a regular amount from your retirement portfolio to supplement your needs. What lifestyle will you have in retirement? Can you sustain that lifestyle?

You've spent a lifetime saving for retirement. Now it's time to imagine your retirement years.

Living in Retirement: Don't Burst the Balloon

I can sum this entire chapter up in a few sentences. Then I will expand on these ideas.

You aim to retire at a certain age. You know you won't live forever, but you want to live comfortably for as long as you live. So you want to take care of your money in a way that can help it outlast you.

I explain more; read on. Feel free to grab your highlighter, pencil and notepad.

Go ahead and plan along.

Living in retirement requires you to think about your monthly budget. It might be tedious. But before you read any further, it's something you should write out. Most of us don't have a written budget. We glide through our best working years making enough to live a life where we can buy what we want. We can plan vacations. We can eat good food.

And if we don't have enough money we get loans and charge up credit cards. (Not always the best solution.)

That changes when our career ends and regular paychecks stop.

If I were a 21st-century retirement algorithm, I would ask you for information like this:

- At what age do you want to retire? (Many should add more years to their imagined retirement age. This can be magnified if you are a low-risk investor. Low risk investing can mean low returns. Low returns in the long-haul can struggle to keep up with your cost of living.)
- How much have you saved for retirement?
- How much are you saving each month?
- How much will your social security benefit(s) be? How about your pensions?
- And how much will you need to spend each month?

Folks stumble with the last question. How much will you spend? It's the budget. You probably spend more time thinking and planning vacations and holidays than you do your budget. Why is that?

Warren Buffett said, "Accounting is the language of business." Your personal budget is the language and blueprint for your comfortable retirement. It's the blueprint that can say a lot about what your retirement could look like. A budget – or lack of a budget – can quickly expose problems. It can help address what actions need to be taken before and during your retirement. For instance, do you want to make room for a mortgage payment every month? Or should you pay off your mortgage before retiring?

Do you think century-old companies would have made it past five years without a budget?

So before you ask if you've saved enough for retirement, ask where your money is going now. This is all relative. I've seen folks who earn high wages. Yet they can't quickly describe where the money goes. I've also seen people who have a high mastery of where their money goes.

Living Well; Below Your Means

Let me ask you, what's the best way to save money on vacation? Travel Websites? Cheap airfare? Spending one day less on vacation?

Nope. Nope. And nope. The answer I'm looking for is simple.

Just spend less in total.

Some examples try to motivate you to plan ahead and spend less. *If you saved one dollar a day* ... You could have 365 dollars saved in a year. So?

Focus on the big picture.

Develop and practice responsible financial habits.

Discover what will motivate you to stay on track.

If your goal is to pay for your vacation before you arrive home from vacation, then save accordingly.

But think about why you want to pay for your vacation before you return home. Because the last time you booked the vacation on a credit card and took 20 months to pay for it? Maybe you spent more than you wish you had? These are strong motivators. That's thinking about your bigger picture.

Living below your means really requires you to recall the big picture. You have to think ahead.

You will always have surprise expenses come up. Count on it.

If you spend more on your home or healthcare in a given month, then cut back in another area. Could this mean you wait until next month to buy something fun?

False Financial Finish Lines

When I observe what I view as *Comfortable Retirees*, they have a few common traits. First, *Comfortable Retirees* pay for their home before retirement. They do not have mortgages. Second, *Comfortable Retirees* aren't forced to take a social security check at a particular age. They draw this benefit when they feel it is right for them. It helps supplement their income. But it does not make up the majority of their retirement income. Finally, *Comfortable Retirees* do not live in excess. They live well and below their means.

The good habits that get you to retirement can get you through retirement.

So drop your bad habits. Examine your habits, if you're serious about living comfortably now and in retirement.

A healthy habit is having a sense of independence from what friends and family do.

We can be deeply persuaded by what those in our lives are doing. This is true when talking about retiring, too. Your friends seem to be retiring lately. Should you?

Your retirement timeframe is highly personal. Wealth is relative. Know what's important to you.

Your Late Retired Years

Retirement planning discusses essential questions about living. Death is also a reality. I'll explain to clients, "Now, you are ... 58? How long will you live?"

A candid conversation about health and their parents usually follows. But the point about longevity risk has been made.

Clients don't walk into my office with their date of death stamped on their forehead. This unknown factor is important.

Your retirement time frame is a significant factor in retirement. And funding retirement becomes more uncertain when the timeframe is unknown.

So how do you strive to spend your money conservatively, so that you have some money left when you die?

If you needed 500 bucks to get you through five limited years of life, then the problem would be pretty easy to solve. You would spend something like $100 per year, right?

How long you will live is an unknown number for most. Technology and science have helped contribute to longer life expectancies. Society, politics, and finance have tried to keep up.

Time. It's incredible how we can hope for a long life. We nod our heads in agreement that healthcare can contribute to a longer life. Yet we do the opposite when spending our dollars.

You may live a long life. But then you go to the social security office and ask for your benefits, earlier, rather than later. You want to retire. You should enjoy life.

Enjoy life on your time. And fuel your retirement with good habits.

Once your regular paychecks stop, you will no longer refill your emergency fund with wages. You may only have a few sources of income. Establish an emergency fund. Keep your emergency fund throughout retirement. This is money you keep in your bank account or available, so you have it when surprise expenses arise.

False Financial Finish Lines

Don't treat your retirement portfolio like a checking account.

How about when your furnace breaks down, and you go to your retirement portfolio? Or you have taxes to pay ... or healthcare expenses ... or you need a different car.

Things happen. But it's always something. So count on it. Keep an emergency reserve that is enough and separate from your retirement portfolio.

Someone who drinks from the well too often will find a dry well sooner rather than later.

Plan for a long retirement.

Clients don't usually tell me that they wish they'd saved less for retirement.

Besides, I'd sooner need a backup plan for having too much, than for having too little. I'd rather have the ability at 100-years-old to be generous.

Aging Gracefully

President Ronald Reagan is famous for many things. A part of what became his story after his presidency is his battle with Alzheimer's. He wrote a letter where he said his thanks and farewell to the nation while he still could do so.

What a hard letter to write. I can't imagine sitting down. I imagine Reagan's loyal spouse, Nancy, at his side. He writes succinctly. He wants to tell the nation that he is not afraid. He writes, "When the Lord calls me home, whenever that may be, I will leave with the greatest love for this country of ours and eternal optimism for its future. I now begin the journey that will lead me into the sunset of my life." (Reagan, 1994).

Good for him. I'm sure that letter had to leave him with a sense of peace. And it certainly did bring awareness to the condition that confronts many Americans. We likely all know someone who has suffered or suffers some form of memory illness.

My Grandpa Tabor saw Alzheimer's Disease set-in during at least his last decade of life. He treated those with mental illness. He retired late in his life. Grandma spent his remaining years shielding him from minor mistakes at first. Those minor social miscues became significant. Once grandpa walked off at a family dinner. The local police helped us find him blocks away.

Eventually, Grandpa moved to the care of a memory unit at a nursing facility. I remember seeing him there. A smile on his Polish face. (He loved that he was Polish and pierogi and his Catholic-Polish Pope, Saint John Paul II.) There was still love in his heart.

It was tough to see the door shut to Grandpa's unit when we left. It was like watching the door shut on me for the first time, as I dropped my son off at daycare. We were helpless. He was under the care of providers and his Lord. I took another peek through the narrow window on the door to the memory unit. Grandpa was already asleep in a recliner.

By the way, these changes for Grandpa didn't come about with ease. The strain of being a caregiver wore on Grandma, I think.

She was strong up to Grandpa's last day and at his funeral. Then something changed. Grandma was diagnosed with Parkinson's. Then came dementia. My grandma, with the biggest heart in the world, was receiving care. First by drop-by caregivers. Then the caregivers were present 24/7. She continued to live in her home throughout her remaining years. The stories remained around her, and the visits continued.

Alzheimer's Disease, Parkinson's, dementia, and ill health in general, can afflict those we love. It forces us outside our comfort zone. Any illness — be it mental or physical — is difficult and calls for an ocean of grace.

I write about the late years of our lives because it's helpful to begin with those final years in mind. How would you want to live? What would you want your family to know? What would you want to say to your community and loved ones if you no longer knew who they were?

When we imagine retirement from our early years through our 50's and 60's, we likely imagine our active years. We'll catch up with friends. We'll play 36-holes of golf and have an early dinner. We'll chase our grandkids around wherever they may be. We'll reignite that passion we had for music, crafts or sports. We'll discover new hobbies like painting.

While you're busy living, consider planning for your late years, too. Now, I have no idea what it takes to age gracefully. I know all sorts of folks that lead examples of what aging gracefully might look like. I've listened to some of those from The Greatest Generation. I've heard inspirational stories about seniors on TV. A great tale teaches aging. *Tuesdays with Morrie* by Mitch Albom is about a man who becomes ill with Lou Gehrig's Disease. An old student who was caught up in the fast pace of life reconnects with his teacher. Morrie speaks candidly about life, joy, pain, and relationships.

So strive to age gracefully. Then write me when you find out what that actually entails.

I have some ideas of what it means. It means deciding and reaffirming early and often that you will accept help from loved ones. That you will cherish the opportunity to relate your experience to any and all who will listen. That you will give up your drivers license.

It means realizing that you have immeasurable worth.

Aging in Stages

The Commission for Financial Capability in New Zealand researched its elder population and defined three phases to retirement and aging. I've seen these three phases described in all sorts of literature. Those stages became Discovery, Endeavor, and Reflection[1].

They defined these stages so they could educate the public about what to expect as an aging New Zealander, concerning money and wellbeing.

The Discovery phase is about exploring your retirement when you are likely healthy and more mobile. If you're fortunate enough, this can last a decade or more. These years tend to be more expensive. If friends ask you to join them on a trip, you're more likely to go. There's no job calendar in your way. You're more likely to catch up with family in and out of state. You may spend more on lunch and coffee because you're out more.

Expenses shift as we age. Health begins to decline gradually. So you stop traveling as much. You stop going out. You depend on your family for more things.

Your children think about your well-being and health. Your declining health is probably an uncomfortable topic for your family to bring up. Do them a favor and bring it up for them. Perhaps you've already decided to move to a senior community that has a college campus-like environment. You have evening movies, shopping excursions, and friendships across the hall.

The Endeavor phase slows you down a bit. You may not travel as much. More of your money goes from paying for entertainment to paying for healthcare needs. It's a time when

---

[1] Commission for Financial Capability, New Zealand. *The Three Stages of Retirement*. https://www.cffc.org.nz/retirement/the-three-stages-of-retirement/

health and age can begin to force tough choices upon you and your family. This phase can see downsizing and proactive moves to senior communities.

Finally, the Reflections stage sees expenses go up further in the healthcare category. This is the stage where help is much more likely needed. You have lost friends. You have new friends. You have a family, and they probably visit you. (Candy encourages the little ones to visit more often.) You share photos to help tell your story.

The pendulum swings from fun expenses to necessary expenses throughout these stages. Expenses swing from entertainment and fun to taking care of yourself.

Of course, this is a study. It is not you. Life happens at its own pace according to our health and ambitions.

Knowing what to expect as you grow old can be a gift. Think about it. If you knew about road construction, you might try to plan your way around it, right? Aging and different challenges might be like road construction. You can take control by planning out several alternate routes.

I mentioned senior communities. I love to hear that a relatively young and active couple is going to move to a senior community or association. These communities have come a long way. Many feel like a college campus experience, or a summer camp, or a daily resort. There are daily activities planned. Peers can relate to you. You don't need to move away when you need more assistance. You graduate to the next level of care.

So much of our well-being seems to be affected by how we spend our time. If I had a choice between a social community or living alone, well, today I think I'd choose a community of peers.

This is all food for thought, right? How can I tell you how you ought to live? That a senior community ought to feel appealing? They have their own costs, too, right? And I'm sure they have their drawbacks.

The end is just the beginning
Become aware of where you are today.
Take the time to imagine your future.
I want to wish you a prosperous life.

If you're fortunate to have your wits about you, a bit of wealth that sustains you, and friends and family that love you, then I think you are doing just fine.

I'll let you know how I'm doing when I get there.

Appendix

Appendix A: Wealth Essentials

A1: The Emergency Reserve

A2: Debt

A3: It Really is the Budget

A4: 7 Rules of the Road

Appendix B: Money Musings For Your Home

B1: Funding Your Little's Education

B2: Calculate Your Retirement & Goals

B3: First Fill up the Water Balloon

B4: My Take on the 4% Withdrawal 'Rule'

Appendix C: Portfolios, Investing, and Butterflies

C1: Round Number Milestones

C2: Age and Risk

C3: Politics and Current Events

C4: Nearsighted Goals

Appendix D: Social Security and Retirement

Appendix – Tipping The Scale of Wealth In Your Favor

This Appendix is like a potluck dinner for financial goals and FAQs. If you've been to a potluck, you know that dinner is always a surprise. You bring enough food for your family, and you share amongst friends and family.

So, what should you bring to this part of the book? Bring a mind full of questions you want to settle for your family. Bring a pinch of curiosity, too.

The Appendix is a collection of ideas that I address often enough that I thought I'd provide written answers here. You can reference specific ideas today. You can dive deeper into areas you read about throughout the book. Or you'll realize there was a bit of wisdom or a hilarious joke that you'll come back to later.

What follows are the luck-of-the-pot ideas. They're common questions and scenarios that affect your life and money. These are responses crafted after a decade of experience.

Many of these ideas are very brief and crisp.

These ideas cover a broad swath of personal finance. You can read about portfolios. You can read more about different distractions.

You might be able to reference this *Appendix* and become more informed. Maybe your life will improve just a bit as a result. Mission accomplished.

May the Scale of Wealth tilt toward your favor.

Appendix A — Wealth Essentials

False Financial Finish Lines

A-1 — The Emergency Reserve

"Beware of little expenses. A small leak will sink a great ship."
-Benjamin Franklin

The captain on a sinking ship surely wishes he could seal the holes.

The patch-kit for your finances is your emergency reserve. Regard your emergency reserve as one of your most essential and versatile assets. Even in the face of high debts, your emergency reserve should be an equal priority.

Cash is King.

There's a saying that sticks. But it's underutilized and under-appreciated today.

Do you know what you'll likely reach for when your family budget springs a leak?

Your emergency reserve.

When you run into lousy portfolio weather, driving your portfolio down in the short-term, do you know what could sustain you?

Your emergency reserve.

What is this emergency reserve?

False Financial Finish Lines

By tradition, it's the money you keep in savings. Don't touch it until you need it.

It ought to be at least one month's sum of your living expenses. You can build up to 3-6 months worth of living expenses. Finally, it ought to be enough for you, so that you are reasonably comfortable — even as life's surprises pop up.

The emergency reserve is an essential piece of your personal prosperity puzzle. Young or old. A new investor or seasoned investor; if you are in debt or debt free. Retired or working. Your emergency reserve can be a valued resource.

If you don't have one, then today is the day you can begin building up your emergency reserve. You may be surprised at the relief and flexibility it can provide.

A-2 — Debt

Money is a bold topic. Conversations about retirement and striving for good outcomes would not be complete without acknowledging debt.

Here's the punchline to debt: Debt exists. It is a number. It can work against you, and it can potentially work with you.

When striving to fund a future retirement, your debts and expenses often get in the way. You have priorities. And usually, your retirement, which is decades away, takes a back seat.

Coordinating your income, debts, and retirement is often a juggling act.

At a fundamental level debt is simple. We start to complicate it when we rationalize it and attach emotions to it. There is not really such thing as good debt or bad debt. There is debt. Then there is no debt.

You can change how you think of debt. This is what I mean when I encourage folks to adopt a healthy perspective of longterm student loans and mortgages. Do you want to repeatedly obsess over longterm loans? Or do you want to incorporate these loans into your wealth story? There is debt. Then there is no debt. You can improve your wealth over time. You can pay off debt in time. Strong financial habits can help you. You can read the *Education* and *Home* chapters to learn more.

We start messing up when we start seeing debt as a free lunch. Or worse. Be careful if you start to rationalize how something happened. Spend less than you make. Live well below your means. Look at where your debt is today and see how you could improve.

Keep debt simple. Make it a number. Seek out guidance from professionals, books, and resources that you feel can motivate you and guide you to improve.

Debt is an example of something that is so unique and affects us all in different ways. That's why the first step in evaluating your debt obligations may be looking inward. Ask how you feel and react to your debt.

Debt guidance is an area where clients hear one thing and do the opposite. It's likely because of how the debt makes you feel. It might make sense to you to pay off your credit card. But you kind of like having your cash in the bank, for example.

If you are married, you may find that you respond differently to debt than your spouse does. Your parents may have an entirely different view of debt.

There is a balance.

Ideally, you will seek an optimal strategy for you. It can allow you to focus on both your near-term and long-term goals. Remember that Scale of Wealth? It's about increasing your assets on one side while removing debt from the other. Increasing your wealth is about momentum. If you pay off a liability, then what happens to your wealth? If you pay off your car loan with your emergency reserve, will the Scale of Wealth move? All you did was remove a vital cash asset. Then you paid off a debt. But your net worth is approximately the same. Instead, think about how your income can help pay off your debt faster. Think about how taking some (not all) of your emergency reserve gets you closer to your goal. Think about how reducing your expenses can help you get closer to your goal. Don't try to tip the scale all at once. Keep your momentum going.

Imagine you had 100 dollars available to pay down debt or save toward retirement. How much of that 100 would you commit to debt payments? How much would you commit to retirement? The optimal answer is likely some of each.

First, there isn't a one-size-fits-all debt payoff strategy — sorry. There are many strategies out there. That's where some confusion and indecision arises. To quote Shakespeare's Hamlet, "To thine own self be true." In other words, follow a strategy that works for you.

Here's a 5-step process you can try:

1. Judge your tolerance for the debt you are assessing: How much stress does this debt cause you? How much does it affect your ability to spend and save money elsewhere? How "normal" is this debt given your circumstances? What would happen if you paid this debt off?

2. Review your debts/loans: How long have you had this debt? What are the minimum required payments? What is/are the interest rates? How long will it take to pay off? Don't rationalize your debt. Look at the debt as debt. It is a number.

3. Evaluate your savings/checking balance: If you had a $2000 surprise bill, could you pay for it without putting that expense on a credit card?

4. Examine your spending and budget. Do you have money left at the end of the month? Does your savings account go up or down over a six month period? Can your budget afford to increase your debt payments beyond the minimum payments?

5. Choose your strategy:
(a.) You can begin with your highest interest rate debt first. You generally pay minimums due on your lowest interest account(s). The extra funds you have in a given month get directed toward the highest interest rate debt. Once this debt is paid in full (Awesome!), then move on to the next highest interest rate debt, and repeat the process.
(b.) You can begin by paying off your smallest balance first. You generally pay the minimum on your other account(s). Extra funds you have in a given month get directed toward the lowest balance. Once this debt is paid (Alright!), then continue to the next highest balance.
(c.) Combo: You may decide that you only have two or three outstanding debts that bother you. Maybe if you paid off these debts, they would help free up your monthly money. So you may commit to a combination of paying off a small(er) balance first. Then you target your highest interest loan.

False Financial Finish Lines

There are a lot of opinions out there on how others think you should approach your debt.

Remember: "To thine own self be true." Do what works for you.

When it comes to your strategy, you may want to discuss your circumstances with your financial advisor or tax advisor.

A-3 — It Really is the Budget

You could make gobs and gobs of money. And you still could make money pros scratch their heads when they look at your family bank. Where does your money go?

That question is one for budgeting.

Budgeting is where you review and discover where your money goes. You make general, flexible decisions about how much you will spend - and on what - in the months and year ahead. A budget should be flexible. A budget is not, however, an endless expense account. It takes discipline to follow a budget.

A budget should allow you to look at costs quickly. You can see where the money goes. For example, how often do you visit restaurants? How much did gas cost last month?

Finally, a budget is a line in the sand. You have a given amount of money you allow yourself to spend on entertainment, for example. If your limit for entertainment is $150 in January, and you spend that much by January 10th, then you have a few options. One option is to look up free things to do for the rest of January. Another option is to trade spending from another area of your budget. Maybe you forgo that new couch you wanted to buy for two more months.

False Financial Finish Lines

Whether you make a lot or a little, sit down and do your budget.

A great place to start is your bank account(s) you use to pay most of your bills. Look at 12-months of statements. Reviewing your statements should give you a good idea of how much you're spending.

Here are some DON'T's:

- DON'T rationalize expenses, or explain a cost away as a "one-time thing."
- DON'T spend the extra money you have at the end of a month or budget period. You know what we call money that you have left at the end of a month? Savings. Save it.
- DON'T operate on a whim. Your budget is not an endless expense account. If a surprise comes up, then this pushes you over budget.
- DON'T be so hard on yourself.

I'll point you to other resources for budgeting. Go to your local library or search online. There are many tools that are available that can guide you through the budgeting process.

A budget helps you recognize where your money goes. From there you can layout goals and see if they are within reach.

A-4 — 7 Rules of the Road for A Comfortable Retirement

What follows are seven rules or principles that I find can apply to life. Life brings many changes. Many are beautiful moments. Other changes can test us. During any journey it's nice to have a map with rules to follow.

Here are seven rules for your financial life journey.

1. Money In: Money Out: Spend time learning about what money will come in. Then study what goes out. Study your primary checking account. Look at the past 12 months.

This can give you a good idea of what goes out. And what you earn.

2. Live below your means: Good habits tend to follow us around. It's never too late to start. Be careful to spend less than what comes in. Also, enjoy that mocha once in a while.

3. Remember, It's Always Something: Dentist bills, car repairs, appliances…you will always have surprises. Keep an emergency savings reserve that is enough for you.

4. Don't Rationalize: Be mindful the next time you make a significant purchase. Too often we buy first and justify later. Marketers are aware of this human behavior. Do your research, write out a pros/cons list, and wait before buying.

5. Two Things. Cost of Living and Taxes: The price of stamps, bananas, and healthcare keep increasing. Taxes may reduce your retirement income. Learn now how taxes and inflation will affect the value of your money throughout retirement.

6. Invest Accordingly: Compounding and math can work in your favor. Consider adopting a long-haul mentality. Know what to expect. Delegate what you don't have the time or passion for – like investing. Inquire about costs, best practices, and how available your money will be.

7. Money is Relative – You Can't Fit Everything on a List: Your circumstances are unique. Life choices are highly personal. Your financial strategy ought to reflect this.

Appendix B — Money Musings for your Home

False Financial Finish Lines

B-1 — Funding Your Little's Education

The monk seal prefers to live alone in two areas on earth. One is Hawaii, and the other is the Mediterranean. There aren't many left along the shores of Hawaii. So if you see them, it's a rare treat.

The monk seals prefer to live alone. So when a momma monk seal has her pup, she defies many mammals behaviors — including humans.

A mom monk seal gives birth on the beaches of Hawaii. They sleep together. She teaches her pup to eat and swim. After 30-45 days, mom says goodbye to her pup. She swims away. After just a short time her pup is on her own.

If you're a parent that has had adult children return home, then you may appreciate the stark contrast to humans.

A college is a place for teenagers to become vibrant adults and a way to leave the nest and prosper. It's been this way for centuries.

A parent's heart and their child's well-being are inseparable. Our love for our children is immeasurable.

This is why it's challenging to coach clients to let their children pay for college.

Examine the pros and cons of paying for your child's college education.

False Financial Finish Lines

I don't believe parents need to be a hero when it comes to college expenses. College is expensive. But it is full of opportunity. It's an ideal place for your child to grow into an independent young adult.

It's a transition for sure. This transition has much to do with why we have a desire to help. We want to support our children.

Part of what I view as a problem is how we frame the conversation about college debt. Let's break these problems into two categories: (1) College costs have increased above the cost of living for decades, and (2) Kids are graduating with high student loan balances today.

First, I'm not going to address how college costs have increased in excess. Many, many colleges need to look at the morality of high tuition. There's a lot of excuses but few solutions. Why should endowments get larger and larger, and yet tuition still increase?

Second, total student loan balances in our nation have increased at astronomical rates for over a decade. The only thing that keeps up with the cost of college is healthcare. College loan balances were under $250 million in 2003. Now they're above $1.2 trillion. (Federal Reserve, Bank of NY). Those numbers translate to many concerned conversations amongst friends and family.

This kind of debt can be the difference between pursuing a dream career or a career that can help pay the bills. For a young family, it can mean buying versus renting a home. Money motivates college graduates. High student loan balances affect lifestyle choices before and after college graduation. It very well applies to you or someone you know.

False Financial Finish Lines

Those are some realities for children. But this debt can also affect you as a parent. Perhaps most important, is how you talk about student loans and money. If you view student loans as a negative, children will pick-up on this. Give them the gift of a mindset to see things differently.

So, let's step back and realize what you are buying – or your child is receiving – when they go to a college. They are buying the opportunity to improve their skills. Their earnings potential increases. Most importantly, they will refine their ability to think independently, and problem solve.

College can be expensive. Listen to college counselors, your professionals, and to your child. Don't overextend your family budget for a 4-year private college, if it doesn't fit. And it may fit.

Think about how the bill is going to get paid. Talk about this process with your child. If you have a high schooler who knows what career they want to pursue, then that can guide college choices. Compare what college experiences feel like and stand back and see what unfolds.

One child may like the idea of volunteering right after college. A child may wish to do something that is likely to provide a moderate income. How will they deal with that?

Unfortunately, paying for college can become a reality for parents too late. Start early.

There's lots of info about FAFSA, 529 College Savings Plans, college expenses, student loans and scholarships available for parents to search online. Please, go search for reliable information.

Underprepared and Ready to Help

But let's assume you aren't as prepared to pay for college as you wish you were. So it's time to fill out that FAFSA and see your children off to college.

I'm assuming that you want to provide something for your child.

So you know, my philosophy is that you need to be honest in evaluating your income and resources. Keep your retirement before your eyes as you explore paying for college. Make sure your retirement is on track.

What can you do?

1. You should follow your child's potential college(s) financial aid process.
2. You should fill out FAFSA – even if you think you're not likely to get a benefit (You may be surprised). Also, don't procrastinate. Fill out your FAFSA as soon as you are able.
3. Review your assets including savings, non-retirement accounts, cash value life insurance, etc.
4. Review loan options made available via FAFSA.
5. Learn how to cover the "family responsibility" gap.

How will you cover the "family responsibility" gap?

All or None ... or Something, rather than nothing? Here are three different general approaches to supporting your college-bound child(ren). Each suggests a different ability and willingness to divert money to your children, rather than your other goals.

False Financial Finish Lines

All

1. **Income**: Income is not the preferred resource for funding because of things like taxes. You work hard to earn your money and taxes reduce your earned income.

2. **Loan**: Who can you borrow from and how much would it cost? What if you did take out a loan or co-sign loans made available through financial aid? Then you have a conversation about how you can afford the payments. Do payments free up your income and ability to fund your retirement?

3. **Cash**: If you have the money, then you may start writing checks for tuition. Before you do so, consider preserving your emergency reserve.

4. **Non-Retirement Investments**: Leave your retirement accounts alone. But you may have an investment account that has accumulated a balance for a rainy day. Could you withdraw some or all this money now?

Something, Rather Than Nothing

1. **You and Your High-Priority Goals**: Retirement Living and Mortgage, etc.: Saving for retirement and paying off a mortgage are high-priority goals. Keep them this way. These should remain high-priority goals for many. A near-term, high priority goal – like college – shouldn't take income and resources away from your long-term goals.

2. **Supplement College Living Expenses**: You may expect your child to walk out of college with debt. That's okay. They exchanged money for something they wanted, right? Meanwhile, you can help in small, but meaningful ways. Send care packages and place random 'Benjamins' in their wallet.

Try to pay for auto insurance, health insurance, gas, food, and books.

None

1. **Rich Aunt?**: Of course, you may always have an aunt or family member that comes through. That kind of feels like a moonshot though, right?

2. **Your Child's Education = Their Bill to Pay**: That's easy for any parent to say, right? (Not likely.) But it does have some truth. You may still co-sign loans. But you set the expectation that this is your child's opportunity to better their life. Study hard, get good grades, and good luck!

Prior to investing in a 529 Plan investors should consider whether the investor's or designated beneficiary's home state offers any state tax or other state benefits such as financial aid, scholarship funds, and protection from creditors that are only available for investments in such state's qualified tuition program. Withdrawals used for qualified expenses are federally tax free. Tax treatment at the state level may vary. Please consult with your tax advisor before investing.

B-2 — Calculate Your Retirement and Goals

When you are saving for any goal, you sometimes want mile markers, so you can see how you compare. The trouble with the goal of living in retirement is that there are many unknowns.

How long will you live?

How will your retirement portfolio fluctuate before and after you retire?

How will your health hold up?

What will the cost of a car be when you need to replace it?

These risks can be reduced (but not eliminated) with a well-funded portfolio. A detailed strategy with goals and defined perimeters may help. The same goes for vacations. An unplanned vacation may sound like a thrill. Most of us like to know what clothes to pack and whether we should bring our passport.

If you don't know where you are going, then any road is an excellent choice, right?

What to Bring

Two or more sources of income will likely fuel your lifestyle in retirement.

False Financial Finish Lines

Social security is a resource for income. A pension is a source of income. Your self-funded retirement account(s) – like a 401(k), 403(b), Profit Sharing, Defined Benefit Plan, etc. – is another resource.

Keep this simple.

There are calculators that you can try to use online. I'll leave it to you to determine if they're reliable or not. You can also read or reread *Chapter 11, Ready, Set, Retire* and *Chapter 12, Living in Retirement.* These chapters expand on this. Hey, you can visit with your professionals, too.

Your retirement plan should start with realizing how much money will come in and how much money will go out. The goal is to have more money coming in from income resources than going out.

So, what will it cost you to live in your retirement?

Add up your money coming in from reasonably reliable income sources. Income comes from sources like social security and pensions. That gets you some income. Then look at what you're expecting to spend. Do you have more income than expenses? That sounds like a good start. Now keep going.

How much will you withdraw from your retirement portfolio to cover the rest of your expenses? Will this withdrawal be sustainable through your lifetime?

Imagine the What If scenarios of life. What is Plan B and C if a wrecking ball goes through your retirement planning? What if a health crisis comes up? What about a prolonged need like longterm care needs?

Retirement calculations are a neutral party. They consider how long you'll live, the cost of living increases over time, and portfolio growth. Retirement forecasts don't always discuss portfolio fluctuations. They more often do not address "What If" crises.

I do not like to settle with a projection or plan. Your retirement is too unique for that. One year is different from the next. Annual reviews can help inform you to adjust, as needed. Carry a pencil.

Carry a Pencil

If you write out your retirement calculations, make sure to use an erasable pencil. The pen could get sloppy in time.

I am a believer in a strategy. A strategy can shift, as needed, and can try to adapt to your life.

Life changes.

And that's a mantra of *False Financial Finish Lines*. I don't think you cross the finish line once you've planned and calculated your retirement out. I have found it's common for clients to ask how they are doing on a regular basis.

It's no different from flight paths. They change with the weather and conditions.

Air traffic and weather can cause you to detour. Do not fear. You can still get to where you are going. But it may be necessary to alter your course.

B-3 — First Fill-up the Water Balloon

A great deal of literature and marketing goes into motivating you to save for your future goals.

Amassing a portfolio to live comfortably is up to you. I've yet to have clients share with me that they wished they'd saved less for retirement.

Accumulating money for retirement is like filling up a massive water balloon. When you retire you poke a hole in the water balloon. You want to allow the money to flow out at a reasonable rate. If the hole is too large, then you risk reaching a low water level. If the hole is too small, then very little water will flow out.

There's a balance between bursting the balloon and being too conservative. I prefer to err on the conservative side.

B-4 — From Full to Flowing:
My take on the 4% Retirement Withdrawal 'Rule'

The transition from saving for retirement to living in retirement can feel uncomfortable. This makes sense. You probably spent little time minding false portfolio milestones. It's fun to see it reach round numbers. But it's not sustaining you. But your attention turns up as reality becomes clear. Your portfolio will be a vital retirement resource. It will help pay for trips to the grocery store. It can bring you and your family on vacation.

So how much should you withdraw? Should you limit your withdrawals or start distributing the money at a particular age?

How fast should money flow from the water well?

The Scholarly Take
If you think the water well and balloon analogy are dumb, then this explanation is for you. The problem of distributing money from your retirement portfolio can be addressed mathematically. This is about distributing your money as a percent of your total portfolio value.

Just imagine it's 2022. You have saved habitually. Your portfolio has grown. Retirement is calling.

False Financial Finish Lines

You expect you'll take 4% from your $2 million portfolio (that's $80,000) your first year. Then lousy portfolio weather visits two months before you retire.

Your $2 million is now zapped down to $1.4 million. What if you lose 10% more? And you planned on taking out $80,000 your first year...

When a portfolio "hits a wall" in retirement, you may need to reevaluate. Then recommit to your long-haul strategy with some adjustments (Guyton and Klinger 2006; Pfau 2011).

But investors prefer simple answers.

How much can you withdraw from your portfolio in retirement?

Have you heard of the '4% Rule?'

In 1994, William Bengen generally said that a ~4% withdrawal from retirement portfolios might be prudent.

You begin with 4% of your portfolio your first year. Then add inflation (cost of living adjustment, COLA) to that initial withdrawal amount each year – kind of like social security.

He considered lousy portfolio weather, age, and portfolio construction.

Some more research suggests a more flexible approach to retirement income (Guyton and Klinger, 2006).

Life and lousy portfolio weather can throw us curveballs. That's why even Bengen emphasized that your circumstances are unique. Consider them before adopting and adjusting your withdrawal rate (Bengen 1994).

A strategy for retirement spending has many factors to consider. So I'll encourage you to speak with your professional advisors to develop a strategy uniquely designed for you.

So what are you waiting for?

False Financial Finish Lines

Here's your invitation to calculate your future.

Bengen, William. "Determining Withdrawal Rates – Using Historical Data." Journal of Financial Planning. October 1994.

Guyton, Jonathon and Klinger, William. "Decision Rules and Maximum Withdrawal Rates." Journal of Financial Planning. (March 2006).

Pfau, Wade. "Which Retirement Spending Strategy Is Right For You?" Blog, Retirement Researcher. November 2016.

Pfau, Wade. "Getting on Track for a Sustainable Retirement: A Reality Check on Savings and Work." Journal of Financial Planning. (October 2011).

Appendix C — Portfolios, Investing and Butterflies

Appendix C could go on-and-on with questions that are borne out of fear and greed. There are many headlines, sound bites, nuances, and friends that cause the under-informed to question their money. Many questions along the way are distractions. So treat them like a distraction. Become informed and keep your eyes fixed on the horizon and your goals.

If an investor isn't wondering about how gold or oil will affect their money, then they're wondering about how the latest legislation or current event will. These concerns are like road trip games.

They make for good questions that can get to valuable points about what your strategy is doing for you in the long haul. But these questions are better for passing the time. I call them, "portfolio butterflies" – or distractions.

An invested and diversified portfolio should fluctuate over decades. At least this is what countless literature tells me. There are investors who get bruised. Fortunately, in many cases, the bruised investors along the road have made mistakes that are avoidable.

I'm going to venture a long-haul theory and suggest that these types of portfolio and wealth building concerns

False Financial Finish Lines

(butterflies) won't hold a lot of weight in a measurable way even 100-years from now.

But people may choose to still pass the time with them.

C-1 — Butterfly #1: Round Number Milestones

Something happens when a portfolio hits round number milestones. It happens particularly at 100,000…200,000…500,000…1,000,000. It's easy math. These are all just numbers. Something in our brain tells us to pay attention.

Why?

I think it's because of the smooth math. If you lose 20% of a $1,000,000, you have $800,000 left. Right? Now if you make 20% on $800,000, you now have…$960,000. Interesting. Losses and gains work differently with your portfolio. So there must be more to the story than round numbers and percent movements.

What's my point?

First, your strategy probably shouldn't deviate much because of reaching a round number. Continue to carry on.

Second, one day the Dow Jones may be at 100,000. (It will undoubtedly fluctuate along the way.) And let's say it's around 25,000 today. I can see the headlines now. What feels more uncomfortable?

(a.) "THE DOW JONES LOST 750 POINTS TODAY."
Or
(b.) "THE DOW JONES LOST 3% TODAY."

False Financial Finish Lines

It feels uncomfortable to hear that the Dow Jones lost 750 points in one day. But if the Dow Jones began the day at 25,000, then the Dow Jones dropped 3%. It's the same. Right? But it can feel different.

Let math and numbers be just that: math and numbers. The purpose of most retirement portfolios is to help pay for things. The numbers can fluctuate. But the goal does not.

Round numbers and percentage movements are portfolio butterflies. Your longterm results yield more meaning. Round numbers may feel important. But they are just easier to count.

C-2 — Butterfly #2: Age and risk

Prudent teaching suggests that an investor may wish to reduce their risk as they get closer to retirement.

I have some questions about this. What if your retirement is 40 years long? What if you have a pension or may not be that dependent on your portfolio money? Frankly, there are a lot of considerations that go into how much risk you may want to introduce to your portfolio. Risk tolerance has more to do with helping you stick to your investment strategy.

With "Appendix C-1, Butterfly #1: Round Number Milestones," I tried to show how losses can affect a portfolio. Let's elaborate. Losses can hurt more than your gains. Read this, again: If you lose 20% of a $1,000,000, you have $800,000 remaining. Right? Now, if you make 20% on $800,000, you now have…$960,000.

Interesting.

20% does not work both ways. In this example, you would have to make 25% on $800,000 to get back to $1,000,000.

This above idea is why paying attention to your portfolio's risk is essential. Investing can surprise you.

Morningstar is a company that provides a great deal of analysis, research, and resources to advisors and the public alike. They publish a report that shares how the average mutual fund did in a particular investment category. They share how that average investment did. Then they share how the average investor of that specific investment did. Guess what? The investor stinks. They realize a lower return than the investment did; during the same timeframe. (As reported by Morningstar's, *Mind the Gap, Global Investor's Returns Show the Costs of Bad Timing Around the World* (2017). They use the example of a 10-year return ending in 2016. They compare how the diversified equity fund does versus the shareholder.)

Why? How is that even possible? One reason is that investors change when things feel uncertain or uncomfortable.

So what? Should you consider taking on more risk? Should you take less risk?

The answer depends on many things that you have going on.

In practice, I also think it has to do with some professional intuition and history.

But it is possible that a 90-year-old and a 25-year-old may have similar amounts of risk in their portfolios. It all has to do with what you're investing for and how committed you are to a strategy.

Some fundamental questions that you can consider are these:

-Are you willing to accept extreme short-term fluctuations in your portfolio?

-What is your portfolio for? College? Living in retirement?

-How long do you have to invest?

-And perhaps most importantly, how dependent will you be on this money?

Everybody's answers will vary. Every investor's circumstances are unique and subjective. So, for this reason, I'm not going to sound the "Rule of Thumb" trumpet. Any decisions you make ought to be tailored to you.

False Financial Finish Lines

C-3 — Butterfly #3: Politics and Current Events

I imagine this conversation below occurring between Your Financial Professional (YFP) and Client.

Client: Hey what's this stuff I hear about over in XYZ Country going to do to my investments?

Your Financial Pro (YFP): That's a good question. Throughout history, different events beyond our control can cause your portfolio to fluctuate.

Client: Yeh but this isn't any normal thing. This is going to be a huge deal. I'm telling you that now.

YFP: Really? What are you hearing?

Client: I don't know. They just say it's gonna get a lot worse.

YFP: Well you can always make adjustments to your strategy. But why don't we give this a few more days and see?

Client: Ok. (Pause.) But you'll call if somethings up?

This is a familiar dialogue motivated by many current events – when they are current. And it's funny because many current events only feel like they remain current for a couple of hours at times.

Do portfolios fluctuate when an eye-popping headline hits? Probably.

False Financial Finish Lines

Can they fluctuate to an extreme? Sure.

A bull market (usually marked by low unemployment, improving wages, and favorable portfolio results) generally ends in excesses. This means that its foundation isn't built on day-to-day headline news and risks. Bull markets evolve.

So does news about specific laws, regulations, debt, geopolitics, etc. keep me up at night? No. And I don't think it should keep you up, either.

A portfolio that invests in any amount of risk should expect some degree of pullbacks. If you invest for the long-haul, then you should have a strategy. You should accept swings in your portfolio over time.

Remember, you may lose inches on any given day, but you can cover miles in time.

False Financial Finish Lines

C-4 — Butterfly #4: Nearsighted goals

Near-sighted goals can distract you from more important things.

A common distraction is becoming too eager to turn a quick profit on an investment.

Let's say you invest $10,000 and it quickly becomes $12,000 in 6-months. So you cash out. But 36-months later your $10,000 would have been $18,000 if you left it alone.

So you find something on some website or hear something from a friend. Maybe the idea has some credibility to it…maybe it doesn't. Regardless, you invest some of your money in the idea. Let's say you make 10% in a short period. Then you sell it. Wow! You just made 10%.

Months later you realize that the same investment is 40% higher than when you sold it. So you hit the refresh button, again. Maybe you invest more. Maybe you don't. This is called "loss aversion." You become so set on not losing money that you become impatient or sometimes reluctant to sell.

This can happen in the opposite direction, too. That so-called "tip" that you invested in loses 50% of its value. Now, what do you do? You persuade yourself that it's not a bad idea. You keep it. Maybe you get some money back. Or maybe you watch the value of the investment go close to $5. Or zero.

False Financial Finish Lines

I know. I know.

Everyone has a friend that has made money trading stocks, widgets, or whatever.

Okay. So I'm boring and old-fashioned and prefer to strive and handle money with prudence…

Appendix D — About Social Security

D-1 — Social Security and Retirement

Social security is the biggest butterfly for aspiring retirees.

Social Security refers to a particular age as your full retirement age. It does not say you need to claim your benefit at this age. Filing for social security is a big decision. It is a valuable resource to help support you while you live in retirement. So this is why I address the topic.

In approaching this topic for this Appendix, I realized that there are far too many variables to try and address social security directly. This is why there are brochures, seminars, webinars, news articles, and conversations. There is no black and white answer.

Much has to do with your dependency on social security and your retirement funds. Then you have to consider your health. Are you married? Were you married? Your circumstances will cause decisions and options to change.

Perhaps you'd like to become better informed before deciding when to claim.

Social security is a benefit that you become eligible for starting in your early 60's. It provides regular check so that it may support you while you strive to grow old comfortably.

False Financial Finish Lines

You probably know that your benefit improves by delaying your claim. But why bother delaying it? A primary goal of delaying is longevity. You may live a long life in retirement. You may be glad you waited and collected a few years of benefit increases, come 20 years from now.

But your strategy for claiming social security can get much more precise. You may experience a significant job interruption or life change. Your health may change. You may decide that you don't want to touch your retirement portfolio yet.

The Retirement Benefit: A Plan or a Mindset?
Will Social Security be around when you retire? Good question. After all, you do not want to miss what you are due.

Citizens look at Social Security with different opinions. One view is as a system that you've paid into during your entire working life. It's a benefit owed to you.

I'm not about to spin into some long idea about how social security is "underfunded and broke." I don't think that at all. There likely will be adjustments made as we go along. That's what happens with many government programs; they adjust. Albeit, sometimes slowly and just in time.

Social Security adds an immense amount of value to many, many citizens. Pundits claim it's in crisis and running out of money?

Others say it's a supplemental program for retirees. It may help sustain you in your later years.

An alternate view is to look at it as something that can help you early on. It may relieve your need to tap into your retirement assets. Good things can happen to assets left untapped for extended periods.

Will it Last?

First, some history.

The Social Security Administration (SSA) was formed during the Great Depression of 1929–1939, to offer some financial stability. And by the way…the Great Depression has not reoccured since then. What about the Great Recession of 2007–2009? It was big. It was damaging. It affected tens of millions. You likely know friends who were without a job during this time. The Great Recession was hard. Fortunately, it did not extend into an economic depression.

Take a look at photos of soup lines or an iconic photograph of a mother after having just sold the tires to the family car. That is real pain that I don't wish to experience.

The SSA was a real solution to a real problem.

The Basics

Do you know the difference between full retirement age, delayed retirement, and early retirement? These terms refer to your benefit and eligibility.

First, forget about the word "eligibility." Purge it from your retirement planning vocabulary.

The second you start considering your "eligibility" at a particular time and age, I think you're seriously prone to "anchoring." It comes back to the discipline and mindset of an individual (Bidewell, Griffin, Hesketh, 2006).

Here is what anchoring may sound like:

False Financial Finish Lines

Your Financial Pro (YFP): "Thanks for bringing your social security statement in."

Client: Yeah. Listen, I was looking at that. Do you think I could be done working in two years?

YFP: Well, you'll be 63 then...?

Client: Yeah. I can start taking social security then, right?

YFP: Well, that's true. Have we looked at this yet?

Client: I'm sick of working. I kind of feel like I just want to be done...You know?

This is a fictitious, but frustrating conversation and idea for someone such as myself to consider. It's frustrating because it's all too familiar.

Read Appendix A-4, 7 Rules of the Road, again. Rule #4 is, "Don't Rationalize."

The client appears to have rationalized their choice to claim social security as soon as possible. They are, "sick of working." They made a choice before they asked. Us humans can make decisions in reverse. In other words, we decide we're going to do something. Then we defend our decision. I do it, too. Just ask my wife.

The other thing that adds to the early retirement age is friends and family.

I imagine this is how that may sound ...

Client's spouse: A friend he hunts with just retired...

Client: That's right! Their guy [financial professional] told them they could retire.

YFP: Okay. Do you know this friends financial situation? How much do they have saved?

Client: No.

YFP: Do you know if they have pensions?

Client: I don't think so ... And it's not like I can't keep working or go back to work.

YFP: Sure. Let's talk about that ...

This couple appears set on claiming social security. And this isn't all wrong. In 2012, about two out of five social security claims occurred around the "early retirement" age[2].

Any claim you make for social security after age 67 is considered "delayed retirement." Any claim you make before 67, is deemed, "early retirement." Currently, according to the Social Security Administration, if you were born after 1960, then your full retirement age is 67.

Still, two out of five claims are made around the early retirement age.

What's the Hurry? What's In It For You if you Wait?
An eight percent total 12-month rate of increase, in SSA terms. That would be the increase you can expect if you were born after 1943. (And I'm pretty sure every one born before 1943, should have claimed by now.)

So this increase to your benefit is calculated on a monthly basis. It is refreshing for a financial guy to see. A monthly increase is compelling. If you wait one month, you get an increase. That feels like a decent reward for a short wait.

---

[2] Knoll, Melissa and Olsen, Anya. *"Incentivizing Delayed Claiming of Social Security Retirement Benefits Before Reaching the Full Retirement Age."* Social Security Bulletin, Vol. 74, No. 4, 2014.

False Financial Finish Lines

If your full retirement age (67) benefit is $2,000 per month, and you wait just six months, then a four percent increase is applied to your Full Retirement monthly benefit. The longest you can keep collecting monthly increases is 36 months. So you cap out your increases at 70[3]. But that $2,000 would become $2,480. It slowly but effectively increases each month you can delay.

But you can claim your benefit earlier.

Early to the Party

Waiting to claim social security can feel like you are leaving money behind.

$2,000 or $2,480 is a reasonable sum of money.

If you see that you are eligible at 62 for $1,400 a month for the rest of your life, you may begin by comparing the cost of waiting. Why wait four years to start collecting about $2,000 a month, when you can get $1,400 a month now?

Some professionals are quick to explain that, if you live long enough, two claim options will eventually catch-up with one another.

The answer is much like the story of the tortoise and the hare. The tortoise is slow to claim his benefit. While the hare is quick to claim his and begin living off his benefit. The tortoise eventually will catch-up and perhaps even pass the hare. Assuming the tortoise lives long enough, of course.

Let's say the hare started taking $1,400 per month at 62. The tortoise waits until 67 when he can claim $2,000 per

---

[3] Social Security Administration. Benefit Planner: Retirement. https://www.ssa.gov/planners/retire/1960-delay.html

month. The hare started enjoying his benefits 5-years before the tortoise.

Even in this hypothetical example, the tortoise does crawl ahead. It takes about 16.4 years with a simple calculation. By simple, I mean that I didn't add any cost of living adjustment to either benefit option. I did not calculate any other factors such as taxes.

So at about 83.5 years old, the tortoise begins to crawl ahead of the hare because he waited. He waited about five years to claim his benefit. And he had to wait for a little over three times that (16.4 years) for his option to take the lead.

You can review what professionals refer to as a break-even analysis. Mainly, how many years will it take for your choice to delay your benefit prove to be worth it?

Again, many variables come to mind when planning for social security retirement benefits. So below is more a list of **DO's** and **DON'Ts**.

•**DO NOT** claim your benefits without considering all your options.

•**DO** be careful of blanket statements. Not everyone claims social security benefits as soon as they are eligible.

•**DO** become aware of your family health history.

•**DO** consider your marital status.

•**DO** consider the value of your retirement portfolio.

•**DO** consider previous marriages.

•**DO** review your options with Social Security.

•**DO** consider all vital details.

•**DO** consider your options with your trusted professionals.

When should you visit with Social Security? If you wish to become informed, you can speak with Social Security before you are eligible.

Your Backstop

Many retirees decide they want to be early to their social security claims. This is a personal choice.

Social Security will likely be around in some form when you retire. It was designed to solve a real need in society. Today that need has transformed into longevity risk. What benefits or assets will support you as you pursue your comfortable retirement?

Reality says that Social Security's Retirement Benefits deserve your attention. Review your benefits before you make up your mind.

References

The below is my attempt to list many sources that I reviewed while composing and reviewing this manuscript.

Bidewell, J., Griffin, B., and Hesketh, B. *Timing of retirement : Including a delay discounting perspective in retirement models.* Journal of Vocational Behavior. 2006.

Commission for Financial Capability, New Zealand. *The Three Stages of Retirement.* https://www.cffc.org.nz/retirement/the-three-stages-of-retirement/

Kahneman, Daniel and Angus Deaton. "*Does Money Buy Happiness?*
A Brief Summary of 'High Income Improves Evaluation of Life But Not Emotional Well Being." Proceedings of the National Academy of Sciences, Early Edition, September 6, 2010.

Kinnel, Russell. "*Mind the Gap: Global Investors Returns Show Costs of Bad Timing Around the World.*" https://www.morningstar.com/articles/810470/mind-the-gap-global-investor-returns-show-the-cost.html. May 30, 2017.

Knoll, Melissa and Olsen, Anya. *"Incentivizing Delayed Claiming of Social Security Retirement Benefits Before Reaching the Full Retirement Age."* Social Security Bulletin, Vol. 74, No. 4, 2014.

Lemon, Doug. Financial Planning Association. *When to Start Collecting Social Security Benefits: A Break-Even Analysis.* https://www.onefpa.org/journal/Pages/When%20to%20Start%20Collecting%20Social%20Security%20Benefits%20A%20Break-Even%20Analysis.aspx

Mischel, Walter. *The Marshmallow Test: Master Self-Control.* Little, Brown and Company. 2014.

Reagan, Ronald. Letter. https://reaganlibrary.gov/sreference/reagan-s-letter-announcing-his-alzheimer-s-diagnosis. Nov. 5, 1994.

Shiller, Robert. *Animal Spirits: How Human Psychology Drives the Economy, and Why It Matters for Global Capitalism.* Princeton University Press. 2010.

Stanley, Thomas J, and William D Danko. *The Millionaire Next Door.* Pocket Books. 1996.

Stanley, Thomas. *Stop Acting Rich.* Wiley. 2006.

Thaler, Richard. *Misbehaving. The Making of Behavioral Economics.* W. W. Norton & Company. 2015.

Thaler, Richard. *Nudge. Improving Decisions About Wealth, Health, and Happiness.* Penguin Books. 2008.

References B-4

Bengen, William. *"Determining Withdrawal Rates – Using Historical Data." Journal of Financial Planning.* October 1994.

Guyton, Jonathon and William Klinger. *"Decision Rules and Maximum Withdrawal Rates." Journal of Financial Planning.* March 2006.

Pfau, Wade. *"Which Retirement Spending Strategy Is Right For You?" Blog, Retirement Researcher.* November 2016.

Pfau, Wade. *"Getting on Track for a Sustainable Retirement: A Reality Check on Savings and Work." Journal of Financial Planning.* October 2011.

www.ingramcontent.com/pod-product-compliance
Lightning Source LLC
Chambersburg PA
CBHW031415210526
45464CB00005B/1892